WRITER-FILES

General Editor: Simon Trussler

Associate Editor: Malcolm Page

File on
STOPPARD

Compiled by Malcolm Page

Methuen, London and New York

A Methuen Paperback
First published in 1986 as a paperback original
by Methuen London Ltd,
11 New Fetter Lane, London EC4P 4EE
and Methuen Inc, 733 Third Avenue,
New York, NY 10017

Copyright in the compilation
© 1986 by Malcolm Page
Copyright in the series format
© 1986 by Methuen London Ltd
Copyright in editorial presentation
© 1986 by Simon Trussler

Typeset in IBM 9pt Press Roman
By 🅰 Tek-Art, Croydon, Surrey
Printed in Great Britain by
Richard Clay (The Chaucer Press) Ltd,
Bungay, Suffolk

British Library Cataloguing in Publication Data

File on Stoppard.–(Writer-Files)
   1. Stoppard, Tom–Criticism and interpretation
   I. Title   II. Series
   822'.914   PR6069.T6Z/

   ISBN 0-413-57280-3 Pbk

Contents

The theatre is, by its nature, an ephemeral art: yet it is a daunting task to track down the newspaper reviews, or contemporary statements from the writer or his director, which are often all that remain to help us recreate some sense of what a particular production was like. This series is therefore intended to make readily available a selection of the comments that the critics made about the plays of leading modern dramatists at the time of their production — and to trace, too, the course of each writer's own views about his work and his world.

In addition to combining a uniquely convenient source of such elusive *documentation*, the 'Writer-Files' series also assembles the *information* necessary for readers to pursue further their interest in a particular writer or work. Variations in quantity between one writer's output and another, differences in temperament which make some readier than others to talk about their work, and the variety of critical response, all mean that the presentation and balance of material shifts between one volume and another: but we have tried to arrive at a format for the series which will nevertheless enable users of one volume readily to find their way around any other.

Section 1, 'A Brief Chronology', provides a quick conspective overview of each playwright's life and career. *Section 2* deals with the plays themselves, arranged chronologically in the order of their composition: information on first performances, major revivals, and publication is followed by a brief synopsis (for quick reference set in slightly larger, italic type), then by a representative selection of the critical response, and of the dramatist's own comments on the play and its theme.

Section 3 offers concise guidance to each writer's work in non-dramatic forms, while *Section 4*, 'The Writer on His Work', brings together comments from the playwright himself on more general matters of construction, opinion, and artistic development. Finally, *Section 5* provides a bibliographical guide to other primary and secondary sources of further reading, among which full details will be found of works cited elsewhere under short titles, and of collected editions of the plays — but not of individual titles, particulars of which will be found with the other factual data in Section 2.

The 'Writer-Files' hope by striking this kind of balance between information and a wide range of opinion to offer 'companions' to the study of major playwrights in the modern repertoire — not in that dangerous pre-digested fashion which can too readily quench the desire to read the plays themselves, nor so prescriptively as to allow any single line of approach to predominate, but rather to encourage readers to form their own judgements of the plays, to set against the many views here represented.

Tom Stoppard is a unique phenomenon among contemporary British dramatists, squatting cheerfully on a fence of his own construction between 'serious' and boulevard theatre, wryly observing and utilizing both. From the first, when he exploded straight from the 'fringe' of the Edinburgh Festival into the prestigious repertoire of London's National Theatre with *Rosencrantz and Guildenstern Are Dead*, he has displayed a refreshing awareness that the theatre can be *fun* — and that subjects as various as metaphysics, moon landings, abstract paintings, and logical positivism are potentially very funny.

As the themes of the plays here documented suggest, Stoppard has, however, moved from an early disinterest in political issues towards an increasing concern with freedom of speech and other human rights. Some critics have suggested that the focus of such concerns upon the Soviet bloc makes Stoppard that rare animal, a thinking playwright who is also right-wing. One suspects rather that his attitude is rooted in a pervasive humanism, and more specifically in his delight in the sheer diversity and eccentricity of human behaviour and response. From *Enter a Free Man* onwards, this has been evident not only in the subject-matter of his plays, but in their methodology — for in his 'nuts-and-bolts' comedies, as he calls such works as *The Real Inspector Hound* and *After Magritte*, Stoppard no less depends upon his audience's willingness to join in intellectual *jeux d'esprit* than his own skill in setting tantalizing dramatic puzzles.

Inevitably, as some of the reviews assembled here suggest, it is possible to take Stoppard *too* seriously: generally, his own comments will serve as sufficient corrective to this tendency, which confuses weight of content with authorial attitude. As he has himself argued, it is difficult to find a 'single, clear statement' in many of his plays: rather, there's a 'series of conflicting statements made by conflicting characters', who 'tend to play a sort of infinite leapfrog'. It's fun in this volume to watch the critics, whether or not they're aware of it, joining in the game.

Simon Trussler

1937 3 July, born in Zlin, Czechoslovakia, second son of a company doctor with the Bata shoe company

1939 Family moved to Singapore.

1942 Evacuated with mother and brother when the Japanese invaded; his father remained behind and was killed.

1942-46 Mother became manager of Bata shop in Darjeeling; Tom went to multiracial, English-speaking school.

1946 Mother married Kenneth Stoppard, army major, and they went to England, where he worked in machine-tools.

1946-48 At preparatory school, in Dolphin, Nottinghamshire.

1948-54 At public school, in Pocklington, Yorkshire.

1954-58 Became a journalist on *Western Daily Press,* Bristol, where his family now lived.

1958-60 Journalist on *Bristol Evening World*, increasingly specializing in theatre and film.

1960-62 Resigned from job, freelancing and writing *A Walk on the Water.*

1962-63 To London, as drama critic of *Scene,* a new magazine which lasted only seven months, during which he saw 132 plays.

1964 Two fifteen-minute radio plays broadcast, and three short stories published by Faber. May-October, sponsored by Ford Foundation to write in Berlin.

1965 Married Jose Ingle: they had two sons, and divorced in 1971. Wrote for BBC World Service 70 episodes of *A Student's Diary*, about an Arab student in London, broadcast in Arabic. *The Gamblers* performed at Bristol University, *A Walk on the Water* on radio.

1966 *If You're Glad I'll be Frank* on radio, and *A Separate Peace* on TV. Co-translation of *Tango* staged by RSC at the Aldwych, and *Rosencrantz and Guildenstern Are Dead* by Oxford Theatre Group at Edinburgh Festival. *Lord Malquist and Mr. Moon* published.

1967 *Rosencrantz and Guildenstern* a success at

7

National Theatre in April. *Teeth* and *Another Moon Called Earth* on TV, and *Albert's Bridge* on radio, winning the Prix Italia, 1968. Also won John Whiting Award and *Evening Standard* drama award for *Rosencrantz*.

1968 *Enter a Free Man* and *The Real Inspector Hound* staged. *Neutral Ground* on TV.

1970 *After Magritte* staged, and *Where Are They Now?* on radio. *The Engagement* on American TV, and briefly in cinemas in Britain.

1971 *Dogg's Our Pet* staged.

1972 *Jumpers* a success at National Theatre in Feb. *Artist Descending a Staircase* on radio. 11 Feb., married Miriam Moore-Robinson, medical director of Syntex Pharmaceuticals and TV personality: they have two sons.

1973 Translation of *The House of Bernarda Alba* performed. Apr., directed for the first time: *Born Yesterday*, by Garson Kanin, at Greenwich Theatre.

1974 *Travesties*, staged by RSC at Aldwych Theatre, a success in June.

1975 *The Boundary*, TV play with Clive Exton. Adaptation of *Three Men in a Boat* for TV. First film script, co-authoring *The Romantic Englishwoman*.

1976 *Dirty Linen* staged. Aug., spoke in Trafalgar Square for Committee against Psychiatric Abuse, and marched to Soviet Embassy to deliver a petition on dissidents' rights.

1977 Travelled to Moscow and Leningrad with assistant director of Amnesty in Feb., and to Czechoslovakia, for first time since early childhood, in June: meets dissident playwright Havel. Publishes four articles on treatment of dissidents in these countries, a concern also reflected in *Every Good Boy Deserves Favour*, a play for six actors and symphony orchestra, and *Professional Foul*, TV play.

1978 *Night and Day* staged in November. Scripted the film *Despair*.

1979 *Dogg's Hamlet, Cahoot's Macbeth* toured in Britain and US. Adaptation of Schnitzler's *Undiscovered Country* at National Theatre.

1980 Film-script of *The Human Factor*.

1981 Adaptation of Nestroy's play *On the Razzle* at National

Theatre.

1982 *The Real Thing*, another major play, successful in London, Nov. *The Dog It Was that Died* on radio.

1983 Translated libretto of Prokofiev's opera, *The Love for Three Oranges.*

1984 *Squaring the Circle*, drama-documentary, for TV. Adaptation of Molnar's play, *Rough Crossing*, at National Theatre.

1985 Co-scripted the film *Brazil.*

The Gamblers

Play in one act.
Written: 1960.
First performed: Bristol University undergraduates,
    1965 (according to Stoppard, in 'Ambushes for the
    Audience', 1974).

'Waiting for Godot *in the death cell — prisoner and jailer
— I'm sure you can imagine the rest.'*

Stoppard, quoted by Kenneth Tynan,
Show People, *p. 60*

A Walk on the Water

Ninety-minute television play.
Transmitted: ITV, Nov. 1963.
Unpublished.

Written for the stage about 1960, then adapted for television, this was eventually further revised and staged as Enter a Free Man *(see p. 25).*

The Dissolution of Dominic Boot

Fifteen-minute radio play.
Transmitted: 20 Feb. 1964 (issued in 'Plays on Tape'
    Series, BBC, 1984).
Published: in The Dog It was that Died (1983).

The unfortunate Boot runs up an ever-larger fare as he taxis round trying to raise the money to pay it — and ends up without fiancee, job, or clothes. Later expanded as the short film, The Engagement *(see p. 29).*

M is for Moon among Other Things

Fifteen-minute radio play.
Transmitted: 6 Apr. 1964.
First performed: Orange Tree, Richmond, 4 Aug. 1977, as one of
    three lunchtime short plays.
Published: in *The Dog It Was that Died* (1983).

*Dialogue of a middle-aged couple who are receiving an encyclo-
pedia in monthly parts. She is aware of how life is passing her by.
They hear of the death of Marilyn Monroe.*

Stoppard's play does not adjust to the stage very well and looks
like a radio play, over-endowed with poignancy.
                        Ned Chaillet, *The Times*, 4 Aug. 1977, p. 10

If You're Glad I'll Be Frank

Half-hour play for radio.
Transmitted: BBC Third Programme, 8 Feb. 1966.
First stage production: with *Albert's Bridge*, Oxford Th. Group,
    St Mary's Hall, Edinburgh, 29 Aug. 1969 (dir. Henry Murry).
First London production: Young Vic, in double-bill with *The
    Real Inspector Hound*, 23 Nov. 1976 (dir. Jeremy James
    Taylor).
Published: with *Albert's Bridge* (London: Faber, 1969); in *Four
    Plays for Radio* (1984); London: Samuel French, 1978 (stage
    version).

*Glad is the voice of the telephone speaking clock. Her bus driver
husband, Frank, recognizes her voice and tries to find her, while
keeping to the bus timetable.*

If You're Glad actually had its origins in a series the BBC were
contemplating, which I don't think ever happened, about people
in absurd jobs which didn't really exist, and the idea of doing one
about the speaking-clock girl occurred to me then. For me, it is

such a relief to get an idea.

Stoppard, 'Ambushes for the Audience', p. 8

All [Glad's] thoughts come out, while she is intoning the hour. Well, there again, I suppose the play must have said something beyond that, God knows what, but whatever it was, it wasn't what I started out with as an intention. I simply liked the central and basic image of the Tim girl being a real person.

Stoppard, quoted in Lewis Funke,
Playwrights Talk about Writing, p. 229-30

. . . an assault on the whole concept of time as the irresistible force that compels societies like ours to trot obediently in its wake. It is a dazzling piece of work, real theatrical Fabergé, juggling excellent but straightforward jokes ('Frank', screams a conductress to the driver who has abandoned his bus to go in search of his wife, 'the passengers have *noticed*') with a constant stream of time-metaphors turned inside out, all spinning round the still, human centre of Gladys. . . . The scenes switch between no fewer than six acting areas, with the cross-references of speech, movement, and lighting all controlled by the inexorable pips.

Bernard Levin, *Sunday Times*, 28 Nov. 1976, p. 38

A Separate Peace

Half-hour play for television.
First transmitted: 'Double Image', BBC-2, 22 Aug. 1966 (dir. Alan Gibson; with Peter Jeffrey as Brown and Hannah Gordon).
Published: in *Playbill Two*, ed. Alan Durband (London: Hutchinson, 1969); and in *The Dog It Was that Died* (London: Faber, 1983).

A man admits himself to hospital although he is not sick: he seeks quiet and routine. But society cannot accept this, looking for clues to his identity.

[Stoppard's 'Introduction' briefly explains that the play was written as a companion-piece to a TV documentary on chess players, but that it 'does not in fact illuminate what I think about chess players'.]

Rosencrantz and Guildenstern Are Dead

Play in three acts.

First production: Oxford Th. Group, Cranston Street Hall, Edinburgh, 24 Aug. 1966 (slightly shorter version).

First London production: National Th. at Old Vic, 11 Apr. 1967 (dir. Derek Goldby; with John Stride as Rosencrantz and Edward Petherbridge as Guildenstern).

First New York production: Alvin Th., 16 Oct. 1967 (dir. Goldby).

Revived: Young Vic, London, 8 July 1974 (dir. Bernard Goss; with Richard O'Callaghan as Rosencrantz and Christopher Timothy as Guildenstern); Lyceum Th., Edinburgh, 13 Apr. 1978 (dir. Stephen MacDonald); Young Vic, London, 16 Oct. 1979 (dir. Michael Bogdanov).

Published: London: Faber, 1967. (This original version continues for 39 additional lines, of which 19 are the three final speeches of *Hamlet*, and the remainder are given to the two ambassadors, in modern dress. From the 1968 edition on, this ending has been omitted.)

The play takes two minor characters who are almost indistinguishable in Shakespeare's Hamlet, *and makes them the main characters. They have been summoned to Elsinore, but do not know why. They are even uncertain of their own identities. There are episodes from* Hamlet, *particularly the players' scenes, but they never understand what is going on. Instead they pass the time talking, flipping coins, and playing word games. In the last act they are on board ship, going to England. They discover that Hamlet is carrying their death warrant, and decide to accept this: at least their deaths will give them a brief moment of identity.*

[The genesis and influences for this play are well documented. The idea came from Kenneth Ewing, Stoppard's agent, late in 1963, at a time when Stoppard was discouraged.] For no reason that [Ewing] can now recall, he brought up a notion he had long cherished about *Hamlet*. Quoting the speech in which Claudius sends Hamlet to England with a sealed message (borne by Rosencrantz and Guildenstern) enjoining the ruler of that country to cut off Hamlet's head, Ewing said that in his opinion the King of England at the time of their arrival might well have been King Lear. And, if so, did they find him raving mad at Dover? Stoppard's spirits rose, and by the time Ewing dropped him off at his home he had come up with a tentative title: *Rosencrantz and Guildenstern at the Court of King Lear*.

Kenneth Tynan, *Show People*, p. 69-70

[In West Berlin in the Summer of 1964, on a Ford Foundation grant, Stoppard wrote this as a one-act verse farce, performed for one night by English amateurs in Berlin. He began a totally different version in October 1964.] What I do remember is that the transition from one play to the other was an attempt to find a solution to a practical problem — that if you write a play about Rosencrantz and Guildenstern in England you can't count on people knowing who they are and how they got there. So one tended to get back into the end of *Hamlet* a bit. But the explanations were always partial and ambiguous, so one went back a bit further into the plot, and as soon as I started doing this I totally lost interest in England. . . . I was not in the least interested in doing any sort of pastiche, for a start, or in doing a criticism of *Hamlet* — that was simply one of the by-products. The chief interest and objective was to exploit a situation which seemed to me to have enormous dramatic and comic potential — of these two guys who in Shakespeare's context don't really know what they're doing. The little they are told is mainly lies, and there's no reason to suppose that they ever find out why they are killed. And, probably more in the early 1960s than at any other time, that would strike a young playwright as being a pretty good thing to explore. I mean, it has the right combination of specificity and vague generality which was interesting at that time to (it seemed) eight out of ten playwrights.

Stoppard, 'Ambushes for the Audience', p. 6

The play *Hamlet* and the characters Rosencrantz and Guildenstern are the only play and the only characters on which you could write my kind of play. They are so much more than merely bit players in another famous play. *Hamlet* I suppose is the most famous

play in any language, it is part of a sort of common mythology.
. . . There are certain things which they bring on with them,
particularly the fact that they end up dead without really, as far
as any textual evidence goes, knowing why. Hamlet's assump-
tion that they were privy to Claudius's plot is entirely gratuitous.
As far as their involvement in Shakespeare's text is concerned
they are told very little about what is going on and much of what
they are told isn't true. So I see them much more clearly as a
couple of bewildered innocents rather than a couple of hench-
men, which is the usual way they are depicted in productions of
Hamlet.

Stoppard, interviewed by Giles Gordon, in *Behind the Scenes*

[Two of the three acts were completed by Apr. 1965, when the
Royal Shakespeare Company took a twelve-month option. This
expired, so the first production was by Oxford students on the
Edinburgh Festival 'fringe'.] The play was done in a church hall
on a flat floor so that people couldn't actually see it. There was
no scenery, student actors. The director didn't show up. Someone
else filled in. I turned up for thirty-six hours and tried to put a
few things right. [After this] I added a scene. Laurence Olivier
pointed out that the section in which they're asked by Claudius
to go and find Hamlet after he's killed Polonius ought to be in
the play. So I went off and wrote that.

Stoppard, quoted in Ronald Hayman,
Tom Stoppard, p. 12, 8

[The Edinburgh student production] It's the most brilliant
debut by a young playwright since John Arden's. . . . Erudite
comedy, punning, far-fetched, leaping from depth to dizziness.

Ronald Bryden, *The Observer*, 28 Aug. 1966, p. 15

[Kenneth Tynan cabled for the rights immediately after reading
this, and within a week the National Th. had bought the rights.]

If the history of drama is chiefly the history of dramatists — and
it is — then the National Theatre's production of *Rosencrantz and
Guildenstern Are Dead* . . . is the most important event in the
British professional theatre of the last nine years. *Rosencrantz
and Guildenstern Are Dead* is the best first London-produced

play written by a British author since Harold Pinter's *The Birthday Party* in 1958.

Harold Hobson, Sunday Times, 16 Apr. 1967, p. 49

Difference between Rosencrantz and Guildenstern
Petherbridge [as Guildenstern] catches perfectly the sort of student who seems ludicrously earnest until you realize that he's genuinely agonized by ideas. Stride [as Rosencrantz], as the slower, more timid, of the duo, builds up a touching sense of their mutual dependence.

Ronald Bryden, 'Out of their World',
The Observer, 16 Apr. 1967, p. 24

The one, in brown velvet and wrinkled woollen stockings, frankly nonplussed, the other, in peacock blue, with a saturnine, self-deflating wit.

Hilary Spurling, 'Prints of the Japanese Buskin',
The Spectator, 21 Apr. 1967, p. 465

The players
The sophisticated artificiality of this production is richest in the players — a grubby, tawdry band, at once weird, outlandish and wretchedly hard up — and comes to a fine point in Graham Crowden's Player King. This gaunt, chalk-white Pagliaccio with carmine lips and downturned mouth has grown from Augustus Colpoys in [Pinero's play] *Trelawney* but with the undertones of that performance distilled and crystallized. Mr. Crowden now has a sardonic authority and, because he is not required to die in earnest, a rare poignancy in the drooping of an eyebrow, in the flick of his bony wrist as he fences in the final duel.

Hilary Spurling, as above

Another neglected chap, the player, who utters a total of 25 words as himself in *Hamlet*, has been expanded into a single personification of all actors at all times. This is the meatiest role in Stoppard's play, a show stopping demonstration, handled with a marvellously engaging bravura by Paul Hecht [in New York]. The part in a sense stands for the whole drama. It observes itself and simultaneously reports back; it is a display of acting and commenting on that acting as it comes to life. The Player is also

Stoppard's instrument for expounding the play's theme: that an artificial death on stage *looks* more real, is easier to believe in, than a death in real life.

Albert Bermel, 'The Unstaging of Hamlet', *New Leader*, 6 Nov. 1967, p. 29-30

The language
[When the Players first arrive] Guildenstern, 'shaking with rage and fright', exclaims passionately at the disillusionment of the chance encounter: 'it didn't have to be *obscene.* . . . It could have been a bird out of season, dropping bright-feathered on my shoulder. . . . It could have been a tongueless dwarf standing by the road to point the way.' The bird out of season and the tongueless dwarf are surely *kitsch*, but are we meant to appreciate them as being symptomatic of Guildenstern's camp vibration, or to enjoy them as poetry? I guess that Mr. Stoppard is hoping for the latter reaction but would settle for the former, and so the former it inevitably is.

John Weightman, 'Mini-Hamlets in Limbo', *Encounter*, July 1967, p. 40

The play's great achievement is in its use of idiom. Elizabethan pastiche would have been tedious, even in a revue sketch. Stoppard gives them modern, slightly stylized, speech which, surprisingly, blends quite naturally with the excerpts from *Hamlet*. These sound like rather archaic court jargon, which, like present-day legal jargon, is easily accepted. Moreover it lends the scenes in question a rarified distinction.

Frank Marcus, 'Theatre: Ancient and Modern', *London Magazine*, July 1967, p. 76

By dramatizing Rosencrantz and Guildenstern's off-stage life in a capering contemporary prose that jacks up into Shakespeare's courtly verse when the excerpts come round, Stoppard vividly suggests the two languages that are native to all of us. One, our own carping, unbridled private tongue with which we question our existence and bitch at our circumstance; the other, the formal and politic language with which we conduct our business in society.

Charles Marowitz, *Confessions of a Counterfeit Critic* (London, 1973), p. 125-6

Stoppard as visible manipulator

Stoppard himself is watching too closely, is too much with us. His two principal figures are not baffled and lost in their own ways. They are baffled and lost in his, speaking his words for him, placarding his thoughts. Thus there is a steady barrage of philosophical finger-pointing: 'Which way did we come in – I've lost my sense of direction', 'What have we got to go on?', 'We're slipping off the map', 'What does it all add up to?'. The effect is to remove Rosencrantz and Guildenstern not only from the fevered life that is rumoured about them but also from the arbitrary play that is surely going to execute them. They stand outside both, ignorant and omniscient at once, intellectualizing for their author. What this ultimately suggests is a Presence in the wings after all, a designer, a dictator, a listening God of some sort – and it tends to undercut the play's own premises.

Walter Kerr, *Thirty Plays Hath November*
(New York, 1969), p. 51

The blurring of life and art

One of the play's soft spots is that it shuffles back and forth between *Hamlet* as a metaphor for life and Hamlet as a symbol of the complexity of art. When Guildenstern is thwarted by a theatrical prop, there is a moment when Stoppard has his artistic metaphor working. There are others too, moments when it seems that Rosencrantz and Guildenstern are aperceptively aware that they are caught up in the logistics of a puzzling drama, as when the former shouts, 'I wish someone would come on!' into the wings or screams, 'Fire!' and then comments sadly, while looking at the audience, that nobody has moved. The old weatherbeaten words of *Hamlet* have never sounded quite so significant as they do coming after the whirlwind word-play that now precedes them.

Charles Marowitz, *Confessions of a Counterfeit Critic*
(London, 1973), p. 125-6

[It is] difficult to see at times on what level the author wishes us to understand his text. The play opens with a long scene in which Rosencrantz and Guildenstern are whiling away the time by spinning coins. The result has been heads in about a hundred throws in succession. This is, of course, a miracle, which is presumably intended to enhance the sense of awe surrounding the summons to the court. Yet these intimations of Someone pulling

strings from the Beyond for an Ultimate Purpose are not backed
up by any metaphysical beliefs. Shakespeare can use the Ghost in
his first scene, because the supernatural was still part of his
accepted stock-in-trade. Eliot and Claudel are on weaker ground
when they introduce miracles into their plays, since stage thauma-
turgy costs nothing and proves nothing, but one could argue that,
being convinced Christians, they no doubt believed in miracles,
and therefore were free, as between Christians, to use the
imagined miracles for poetic effect. But Mr. Stoppard's miracle
is a sort of *hors d'oeuvre*, a mere incidental theatrical gimmick,
which gives an excuse for some mildly entertaining back-chat and
funny stage-business, but has no significance beyond itself.
John Weightman, as above, p. 39

Much of the humour is predicated on the dilemma of someone
who wants to get on with his daily business but who must first
deal with the grotesque behaviour of people created by a poet's
imagination. And finally, there is the band of players, the chief of
whom is always discoursing, in a somewhat threatening manner,
on the arts of the stage. All of this, far from enhancing or deep-
ening Stoppard's play, seemed to me just to get in the way.
Jack Richardson, 'Two New Plays', *Commentary*,
Dec. 1967, p. 83

Possible sources and influences
The text abounds in allusions. At times it seems as if he has put
Waiting for Godot inside *Hamlet*, and one admires the courage of
a young man who has the nerve to do this. His characters needle
each other in a vacuum, like the imprisoned souls in *Huis Clos*.
Their prose is occasionally disguised Eliotish verse, with a note of
ponderous, philosophical inquiry which may, or may not, be
taking itself seriously. . . . The stage business becomes remin-
iscent of the mirror-like complexities of Genet, when the Players
put on for them a play within the play within the play.

John Weightman, as above, p. 38

[The players are used] as both Fates and chorus, accelerating
time by jumping ahead in their narrative, rather as Giraudoux
used his gods and gardeners. That's the tradition of drama which
Stoppard has finally imported to Britain: the Continental genre
of modernized myth, on the lines of *Ondine* and *Electra*, Sartre's

Flies and Cocteau's *Infernal Machine*. It's never caught on here before; possibly because we've never had a playwright of their calibre, perhaps because we lacked a mythology we could recognize as compellingly our own.

Ronald Bryden, as above

The genre — literary re-creation and conjecture — was popular on the Continent before the war. Giraudoux explored Greek mythology to point modern morals; among lesser writers, Gaston Baty re-interpreted the story of Don Quixote in *Dulcinea*; Leo Ferrero, in *Angelica*, attacked fascism by using the figures of the Commedia dell'Arte.

Frank Marcus, as above, p. 77

Some negative reviews
The philosophical implication — strutting our brief hour upon the stage, etc. — is banal; dramatically it's self-destructive. We might as well go to the theatre, count up to 10,000, and go home again. A creative exploration of Rosencrantz and Guildenstern, building on Shakespeare's meagre foundations, would have made the play less fashionable, but vastly more entertaining.

Frank Marcus, as above, p. 76

In outline, the idea is extremely ingenious; in execution, it is derivative and familiar, even prosaic. As an artist, Stoppard does not fight hard enough for his insights — they all seem to come to him, prefabricated, from other plays — with the result that his air of pessimism seems affected, and his philosophical meditations, while witty and urbane, never obtain the thickness of *felt* knowledge. Whenever the play turns metaphysical, which is frequently, it turns spurious, particularly in the author's recurrent discourses upon death. . . . There is, in short, something disturbingly voguish and available about this play, as well as a prevailing strain of cuteness which shakes one's faith in the author's serious intentions.

Robert Brustein, *The Third Theatre* (London, 1970), p. 150-1

Two revivals with different emphases
The director at the Lyceum, Edinburgh, has invested Rosencrantz and Guildenstern with very palpapable, not to say

poignant reality as two lost boys in a big black inimical empty space. In addition, the production reduces the impact of Shakespeare's *Hamlet* court, in its brief but crucial appearances, to a parcel of gaudy puppets you wouldn't care if you never saw again. The result is to emphasize, more forcibly than Stoppard's brilliant and scintillating play can easily stand, a comparison between R. and G. and Beckett's two tramps. In other words, it's like a wordier *Waiting for Godot* plus highly coloured interruptions. For me this is a wrong-headed approach (though there's little doubt that the rapturous first-night audience would disagree). Did Stoppard really intend to turn the tables on Shakespeare to this extent? Didn't he really mean to emphasize — whether with allegorical intentions or no — the essentially peripheral role of Rosencrantz and Guildenstern in some incomprehensible but clearly exciting grand plan? Surely it's a confined, insignificant space in which they are left waiting?

Cordelia Oliver, '*Rosencrantz and Guildenstern*',
The Guardian, 15 Apr. 1978

Bogdanov's production [Young Vic, 1979] has a couple of drawbacks. One is that Rosencrantz and Guildenstern (Michael O'Donoghue with a northern accent, Bev Willis with a 'posh' one) are far too unlike to be perpetually confused with each other; and the other is that, if the extracts from *Hamlet* itself are outrageously guyed, as here, then the contrast between the grandeur of the tragedy and the comedy of those involuntarily swept up into it, is forfeited.

Francis King, 'Two Lords A-leaping',
Sunday Telegraph, 21 Oct. 1979, p. 14

A selection of other articles and reviews

William Babula, 'The Play-Life Metaphor in Shakespeare and Stoppard', *Modern Drama*, XV (1972), p. 279-81.

Clive Barker, 'Contemporary Shakespearian Parody in British Theatre', *Shakespeare Jahrbuch* (Weimar), CV (1969), p. 104-20

Normand Berlin, '*Rosencrantz and Guildenstern Are Dead*: Theater of Criticism', *Modern Drama*, XVI (1973), p. 269-77.

Peter Carroll, 'They Have their Entrances and their Exits', *Teaching of English*, XX (1971), p. 50-60.

Ruby Cohn, *Modern Shakespeare Offshoots* (Princeton, N.J.: Princeton University Press, 1976), p. 211-18.

Douglas Colby, *As the Curtain Rises* (Rutherford, N.J.: Fairleigh Dickinson University Press, 1979), p. 29-45.

Manfred Draudt, 'Two Sides of the Same Coin, or the Same Side of Two Coins', *English Studies*, LXII (1981), p. 348-57.

Robert Egan, 'A Thin Beam of Light; the Purpose of Playing in *Rosencrantz and Guildenstern Are Dead*', *Theater Journal*, XXXI (1979), p. 59-69.

John Elsom, ed., *Post-war British Theatre Criticism* (London, 1981), p. 186-91.

C.J. Gianakaris, 'Absurdism Altered: *Rosencrantz and Guildenstern Are Dead*,' *Drama Survey*, VII (1968-69), p. 52-8.

William E. Gruber, 'Wheels within Wheels, etc.: Artistic Design in *Rosencrantz and Guildenstern Are Dead*', *Comparative Drama*, XV (1981-82), p. 291-310.

Helene Keyssar-Franke, 'The Strategy of *Rosencrantz and Guildenstern Are Dead*', *Educational Theatre Journal*, XXVII (1975), p. 85-97.

Axel Kruse, 'Tragicomedy and Tragic Burlesque: *Waiting for Godot* and *Rosencrantz and Guildenstern Are Dead*', *Sydney Studies in English*, I (1975-76), p. 76-96.

R.H. Lee, 'The Circle and its Tangent', *Theoria*, XXXIII (Oct. 1969), p. 37-43.

Jill L. Levenson, '*Hamlet* Andante/*Hamlet* Allegro: Tom Stoppard's Two Versions', *Shakespeare Survey*, XXXVI (1983), p. 21-8.

Geoffrey Morgan, ed., *Contemporary Theatre* (London, 1968), p. 97-103.

J.C. Nitzsche, 'McLuhan's Message and Stoppard's Medium in *Rosencrantz and Guildenstern Are Dead*', *Dutch Quarterly Review*, X (1980), p. 32-40.

Charles H. Salter, '*Rosencrantz and Guildenstern Are Dead*', *Insight IV: Analyses of Modern British and American Drama*, ed. Hermann J. Weiand (Frankfurt: Hirschgraben, 1975), p. 144-50.

Simon Varey, 'Nobody Special: on *Rosencrantz and Guildenstern Are Dead*', *Dutch Quarterly Review*, X (1980), p. 20-31.

Robert Wilcher, 'The Museum of Tragedy: *Endgame* and *Rosencrantz and Guildenstern Are Dead*', *Journal of Beckett Studies*, IV (1979), p. 43-54.

Judith Zivanovic, 'Meeting Death Already There; the Failure to Choose in Stoppard's *Rosencrantz and Guildenstern Are Dead*', *Liberal and Fine Art Review*, I (1981), p. 44-56.

Teeth

Half-hour television play.
Transmitted: 7 Feb. 1967.
Published: in *The Dog It Was That Died* (1983).

A dentist revenges himself on the man having an affair with his wife when he comes to him as patient. To complicate it, the dentist is having an affair with the patient's wife.

Another Moon Called Earth

Half-hour television play.
Transmitted: 28 June 1967.
Published: in *The Dog It Was That Died* (1983).

The day of the parade to celebrate the return of the first man on the moon (two years before the actual first moon landing). Because of his moon walk, 'everything we live by [is] suddenly exposed as nothing more than local customs – nothing more – because he has seen the edges where we stop, and we never stopped anywhere before'. Bone, an absent-minded historian, has to cope with his realization that his wife has taken to her bed so as to receive a fake doctor there, and that she has pushed her old nanny out of the window because the nanny always beat her at games. Nearly all these themes are developed later in Jumpers.

It seemed to me rather pretentious. Does it really need an astronaut on the moon to destroy a silly vain girl's moral sense? Well, it might, but it made an improbable fable, and the language, and in consequence the acting, had something of the fussy dated quality of Christopher Fry. Come to that, so did the title.

George Melly, *The Observer*, 2 July 1967, p. 19

This was a morality play asking the viewer if our earthly values will still be considered absolute when space travel shows us just what a little celestial village we are. Penelope (Diane Cilento)

23

takes the view that our absolutes are mere tribal customs while her husband Bone (John Wood) is a logician who believes in the logical pattern of history. Unfortunately, Stoppard's brave new moon stance wasn't argued with enough earthbound tribal logic.

Stanley Reynolds, *The Guardian*, 29 June 1967, p. 6

Albert's Bridge

Play for radio.

First transmitted: BBC Third Programme, 13 July 1967 (dir. Charles Lefeaux).

First stage production: Oxford Th. Group, Edinburgh Festival, 29 Aug. 1969.

First London production: King's Head, Autumn 1976 (dir. Christopher Selbie).

Published: with *If You're Glad* (London: Faber, 1969); separately, 1970; and in *Four Plays for Radio* (1984).

[Albert] has turned down a future in father's firm, preferring the perspective that comes from a career spent painting a suspension bridge. Albert has had an education, against Dad's better judgment, and all it has done is to make him think about things. Mr. Stoppard's people think furiously, their soliloquies rooted in a painstaking desire to know what's going on. Albert looks down on a toy world and makes sense of it simply by having escaped it. It's left to a would-be suicide who joins him periodically to remark that 'somewhere there's a lynch-pin that once removed would collapse the whole monkey-puzzle.' Then technology strikes, in the ludicrous shape of a decision by bumbling town-councillors. When 1,799 painters move in to help Albert, the result of the Bridge Committee's re-re-calculation of its steel-paint-time-and-manpower equation, the painters' marching feet set up a vibration that collapses the bridge, and with it Albert's precious sense of perspective. Tomorrow's world wins, but you couldn't help laughing.

Paul Ferris, 'Views from the Bridge',
The Observer, 23 July 1967, p. 19

The opening sequence [at the King's Head] established both

scale and perspective by making actors, closely clustered together, shout to each other as if they were vertically a long way apart. After that, a small ladder could stand in quite adequately both for the bridge and for the Eiffel Tower, and the simplicity of the staging was almost always advantageous. Five of the seven actors had two parts each. . . . It was good to limit the sound effects to those that could be produced vocally.

Randall Craig, 'Plays in Performance: Experimental',
Drama, Winter 1976, p. 60

Enter a Free Man

Play in two acts, adapted from the television play *A Walk on the Water* (see p. 10).
First production: St. Martin's Th., London, 28 Mar. 1968
(dir. Frith Banbury; with Michael Hordern as George).
First New York production: St. Clement's Church, 17 Dec. 1974.
Published: London: Faber, 1968.

George Riley is the 'free man', free only in his local pub and then only when able to feel hopeful. Every Saturday he walks out on his wife and, though he abandons his flight later in the day, each week he is convinced that this time it is final. As an inventor, his creations include an envelope with gum on both sides of the flap so that it can be used twice, a clock connected to a tape-recorder so that it plays 'Rule Britannia' after striking, and indoor rain, an arrangement of pipes from a valve and sponge on the roof that makes his living-room look 'like a ship's engine room'. His four drinking cronies – a businessman, a shy young sailor, a good-time girl, and her gambler boy friend – enjoy George's company but gradually see his shortcomings. For half the play George is seen at home with his daughter, who patiently gives him ten shillings a week pocket money from her earnings at Woolworths, and his wife, who adopts the tolerant tone of one dealing with a child too young to do any better. The daughter sets off to Scotland with a boy, but an accident reveals that he is married, and she is soon back, too. The play ends as the room is soaked by the success of the indoor rain, which the daughter tenderly collects in buckets. George finally decides that he will follow her urging and draw unemployment benefit, abandoning his claim to be a self-employed inventor.

It was, in fact, *Flowering Death of a Cherry Salesman.* I can't remember now whether I'd seen [Robert Bolt's] *Flowering Cherry* when I wrote it or not. Sometimes I say I had, sometimes I say I hadn't, in each case believing it. . . . It was about some people I had seen in other people's plays; I didn't know any of them. . . . I would not be dumbfounded to discover that most first plays consist of a writer just clearing the decks by getting his admirations out of the way.

> Stoppard, quoted by Mark Amory in 'The Joke's the Thing',
> *Sunday Times Magazine*, 9 June 1974, p. 68

Formally, it's a fairly cautious exercise in comic nonconformity. Where it differs from such white-collared Broadway celebrations of holy kookery as *The Remarkable Mr. Pennypacker* is that, having claimed off-beat genius for its protagonist, it proceeds to demonstrate it. . . . George is a splendid, full-fledged comic creation, a dynamo of theatrical energy spraying his fantasies and paranoias over the stage like rainbow carnival streamers. . . . *Enter a Free Man* confirms most of the things one hoped that Stoppard's second play would confirm. It bears out that his flair for language and turning ideas on their heads is genuine and original − 'If it weren't for inventors', a character encourages George, with strict but apocalyptic logic, 'there'd be nothing but people standing about getting rained on.' . . . To [George], the alternatives to reality are equally real: he is a genuinely free man.

> Ronald Bryden, 'Follow-up Debut',
> *The Observer*, 31 Mar. 1968, p. 31

The Real Inspector Hound

Play in one act.
First London production: Criterion Th., 17 June 1968
    (dir. Robert Chetwyn; with Richard Briers as Moon and
    Ronnie Barker as Birdboot).
First New York production: with *After Magritte*, Th. Four,
    23 Apr. 1972 (dir. Joseph Hardy).
Revived: with *After Magritte*, Dolphin Co. at Shaw Th.,
    6 Nov. 1972 (dir. Nigel Gordon); with *If You're Glad I'll*

be Frank, Young Vic, 23 Nov. 1976.
Published: Faber, 1968; revised ed., 1970.

Two theatre critics are attending a first night, one for a 'quality' paper the other for a popular one. Moon likes airy-fairy speculation while Birdboot is down-to-earth. They munch chocolates and chase actresses, speaking their notices. Stoppard scores off actors and playwrights, supplying some of the fifth-rate thriller they are watching, with its cliché parts and situations. The radio is switched on conveniently to provide police messages, the exposition could hardly be more clumsy, and the comic char (Mrs. Drudge) answers the phone with 'The Drawing-room of Lady Muldoon's country residence one morning in early spring'. Eventually Stoppard brings his two critics into the play, one stepping forward when the ringing phone on the stage is not answered. The performers repeat lines heard earlier, but they have a new meaning as the reviewers grapple with the 'real' situation in which they are now involved. Finally the critics are murdered.

The one thing that *The Real Inspector Hound* isn't about, as far as I'm concerned, is theatre critics. I originally conceived a play, exactly the same play, with simply two members of an audience getting involved in the play-within-the-play. But when it comes actually to writing something down which has integral entertainment value, if you like, it very quickly occurred to me that it would be a lot easier to do it with critics, because you've got something known and defined to parody. So it was never a play *about* drama critics. If one wishes to say that it is a play about something more than that, then it's about the dangers of wish-fulfilment. But as soon as the word's out of my mouth I think, shit, it's a play about these two guys, and they're going along to this play, and the whole thing is tragic and hilarious and very, very carefully constructed. I'm very fond of the play because I didn't know how to do it. I just got into it, and I knew that I wanted it somehow to resolve itself in a breathtakingly neat, complex but utterly comprehensible way. . . . I didn't know that the body was Higgs, and I didn't know that Magnus was going to be Puckeridge. I mean, as soon as I realized the body had to be Higgs and, later, Magnus had to be Puckeridge, as solutions to the problems in writing that play, it made sense of all the things I'd been trying to keep going.

Stoppard, 'Ambushes for the Audience', p. 8

Perhaps it was much too clever for most of the critics to see at a single viewing — a wonderful Chinese puzzle of a play, and desperately funny as well.

Robert Chetwyn, director of first production, quoted by
Frank Cox, 'Directors in Interview', *Plays and Players*,
Feb. 1969, p. 51

The Real Inspector Hound is I believe only challenged by Peter Shaffer's *Black Comedy* in the post-war realm of minor theatrical classics. . . . In its intricacy and its ambition (a jovial attack on drama critics is grafted onto a parody of an Agatha Christie thriller) and in its sheer hilarity it seems to me a wonderfully successful treat. . . . What follows is a masterpiece of mixed metaphors, mistaken identities, and contorted revelation, but Stoppard's final triumph is that in the closing five minutes he can actually make retrospective sense not only of the previous five but also of the entire play.

Sheridan Morley, 'Happy Returns', *Punch*, 1 Dec. 1976, p. 1043

On one level, there's a light-hearted send-up of critical styles, ethical-pompous and philistine-plainspoken. . . . Next, there's a witty, Goonish caricature of *The Mousetrap*. . . . Finally, there's a parody of *Rosencrantz and Guildenstern* itself. The two critics disappear into the murky doings at Muldoon manor like plain-clothes versions of the hapless lords-attendant of Elsinore. If you liked, you could argue that the play, behind its frivolity, juggled with ideas as serious as the earlier one: that the triple-layered logics Stoppard plays against each other like a multi-dimensional chess master stand for the relativist, anthropology-based world-view of Levi-Strauss and the French structuralists. Myself, I suspect that Stoppard uses them only for the lightning release of humour when logics collide — that, and the comic escape of seeing someone else swallowed up by the universal nightmare of slipping out of ordered experience into chaos.

Ronald Bryden, 'A Critics' Nightmare', *The Observer*,
23 June 1968, p. 26

Neutral Ground

One-hour screenplay.
Transmitted: Granada TV, 2 Dec. 1968.
Published: in *The Dog It Was that Died* (London: Faber, 1983).

Philo, 'a used-up spy without a country', is stranded in a small central European nation, unable safely to travel East or West. He is identified by his pet monkey, and hunted by gunmen, Laurel and Hardy, while an English toy salesman, Acheson, and his wife also become involved in the case. Philo knows 'there are no neutral corners in this world, not for you'. Stoppard's 'Introduction' briefly explains that his play follows Sophocles' Philoctetes *and was written for a series based on myths, which in fact never occurred.*

Neutral Ground did not even have the advantage of personal subject-matter or angle of vision. It was just a very routine addition to the cycle of downbeat, John Le Carre-type spy dramas, about an ageing and drunken ex-spy living abroad and a younger agent sent out to trap him into returning home. It was quite neatly plotted and well acted by Patrick Magee and Nicholas Pennell.

> John Russell Taylor, 'TV Drama', *Plays and Players*,
> Feb. 1969, p. 12

The Engagement

Film (45 mins.), expanded from the radio play *The Dissolution of Dominic Boot* (see p. 10).
Transmitted: NBC, 'Experiment in Television', 14 Mar. 1970, and released to some British cinemas, Aug. 1970 (dir. Paul Joyce, starring David Warner, music by John Dankworth).
Unpublished.

A young man, just engaged, spends all afternoon riding round in a taxi becase he can't pay the fare. Each time he obtains some money the meter has clicked up just beyond what he has. His bank won't help, his office colleagues have just spent their money on a huge, ugly ornament as an engagement present for him, he smashes his gas meter and has too little, he collects bottles to take to the pub, then breaks some. His mother uses his taxi but pays only her share of the fare, a gambling friend might help with a big debt but isn't interested in a little one, then the taxi is used by the police in a chase, and towed away from outside the police station while he is inside. He donates blood for money several times, finally sells all his furniture and clothes, returns to work in his pyjamas and is sacked, and, weak and ill, is put into the same taxi by a well-meaning colleague.

For one reason or another, whenever I have had an idea to write, it's never really occurred to me to write it as a film. A play is something which happens behind closed doors between con-senting adults; and a film is a kind of three-ring circus, and the director is the elephant act, and the writer is a sort of clod who comes in afterwards and clears up the mess. . . . One wants to be in a position to protect one's work, because with the best play in the world one must say that, given an optimum situation – the ideal director, the best possible casting, the best possible set up in the theatre – you will end with something like 70 per cent of what you meant. For 30 per cent of the time you are running around saying, 'That's not what I meant at all; it's all in my head but I can't do it for you, and you just haven't got it'. With a film, a writer hasn't even got a sort of casting vote. At least this is a fixed idea I have about film-making. I don't know whether this is being extremely naive or extremely cynical.

Stoppard, 'I'm Not Keen on Experiments',
New York Times, 8 Mar. 1970, Sec. II, p. 17

After Magritte

Play in one act.
First London production: Ambiance Lunch-Hour Th. Club
   at Green Banana, 9 Apr. 1970 (dir. Geoffrey Reeves).
First New York production: with *The Real Inspector Hound*,
   Th. Four, 23 Apr. 1972 (dir. Joseph Hardy).
Revived: with *The Real Inspector Hound*, Shaw Th., 6 Nov. 1972
   (dir. Nigel Gordon).
Published: London: Faber, 1971.

*The play takes place in a home where people seem to be logic-
ally pursuing a bizarrely routine existence. A mother-in-law plays
the tuba, and a husband and wife getting ready to go out and
perform their dance act carry on oblivious of the eccentric images
they present. They have been arguing about a strange sight they
saw – a white-bearded, one-legged football player hopping down
the street in striped pyjamas – when a detective enters to
question them about a crime he suspects them of having committed. The detective's pursuit of his own inquiry ingeniously
leads to an explanation of both the crime and the couple's appar-
ition.*

Henry Hewes, 'Summer Solace', *Saturday Review*,
26 Aug. 1972, p. 66

It was based on fact for a start – somebody I know had a couple
of peacocks in the garden, and one escaped while he was shaving.
He chased it and he had to cross a main road to catch it, and he
was standing in his pyjamas with shaving cream on his face
holding a peacock when the traffic started going by. This was one
of those moments when somebody tells you something and you
realize that in due course it's going to be useable, so I built it up
forwards and backwards between the first image and the last
image.

Stoppard, 'Ambushes for the Audience', p. 17

[Stoppard adds] that when he tried the peacock anecdote out on
members of a literary society at Eton College, it was received in
bewildered silence. He soon realized why: 'They all *had* peacocks.'

Kenneth Tynan, *Show People*, p. 45

When I encountered [Magritte's] paintings I responded to their
humour immediately and I enjoyed his jokes and I also liked the
fact that he painted things very carefully. You know he combined two things really, he had a sense of humour which appealed
to me, a sense of the absurd if you like, but I also like the way he
did things very carefully and perfectly. . . . You know his famous
jokes, I suppose, the easel standing in front of an open window
and the painting on the canvas simply reproducing what the
canvas obliterates; that sort of thing appeals to me a lot, his jokes

31

about mirrors, his jokes about scale.

Stoppard, interviewed by Joost Kuurman,
Dutch Quarterly Review (1980), p. 56

His pyrotechnic display of repartee, as in *Rosencrantz*, is still in evidence, but in this short play he has gone wholeheartedly for absurdist theatre. The Magritte (fondly referred to by the Mother as Maigret) influence affects the whole play. The fruit bowl hanging from the other end of the light in Magritte fashion, immediately set the atmosphere for the piece. Whether or not there were any profound implications, the audience was constantly heartened by the characters' incredible words and antics.

Randall Craig, *Drama*, Summer 1970, p. 36-7

Article
Leonard Goldstein, 'A Note on Tom Stoppard's *After Magritte*', *Zeitschrift fur Anglistik und Amerikanistik*, XXIII (1975), p. 16-21.

Where Are They Now?

Play commissioned by BBC Schools Radio (35 mins.).
Transmitted: 28 Jan. 1970 (prod. Dickon Reed).
Published: with *Artist Descending a Staircase* (London: Faber, 1973); and in *Four Plays for Radio* (London: Faber, 1984).

A comedy intercutting school dinner in 1945 with the Old Boys' dinner in 1969. All the familiar boarding-school world – of games, nicknames, classes, teachers' sarcasm – is present, alongside the forms it takes in the 'adult' world.

A very slight piece about a school reunion which makes quite ingenious play with different eras coexisting in memory and association. . . . It is cleverly done, but seems to have little to say beyond the most superficial evoking of a widely shared experience.

John Russell Taylor, *The Second Wave*
(London, 1971), p. 103

Dogg's Our Pet

Play in one act.
First production: Inter-Action at the Almost Free Th., London,
7 Dec. 1971 (dir. Ed Berman).
Published: in *Ten of the Best*, ed. Ed Berman (London:
Inter-Action Imprint, 1979), p. 79-94.

*Commissioned by Ed Berman, the play's title is a semi-private
joke, as Dogg's Troupe was one of Berman's many activities and
'our pet' is an anagram of Troupe. A workman and two schoolboys build a platform for a school opening ceremony, performed
by the Queen. The work plays with a kind of code language,
where words have different meanings from their standard ones,
but are used logically. Very slightly adapted, the play became the
opening of* Dogg's Hamlet *in 1979 (see p. 65).*

Simply a lunatic parody of a stiffly-formal, regally-attended
opening ceremony. An overalled workman mutinously constructs
a rostrum out of planks, bricks, and cubes hurled at him from the
wings; a headmaster figure, playing Hardy to his Laurel, kicks
him about like a sausage balloon; and the royal personage arrives
to perform the ceremony delivering a series of rudely abrupt
monosyllables before announcing, with marvellous irrelevancy,
'Sod the pudding club'.

Michael Billington, 'Stoppard',
The Guardian, 9 Dec. 1971, p. 10

Jumpers

Play in two acts and a coda.
First London production: National Th. at the Old Vic, 2 Feb.
1972 (dir. Peter Wood; with Michael Hordern as Moore and
Diana Rigg as Dotty).
First New York production: Billy Rose Th., 22 Apr. 1974
(dir. Peter Wood; des. Josef Svoboda; with Brian Bedford
as Moore and Jill Clayburgh as Dotty).
Revived: National Th. at Lyttelton, 21 Sept. 1976
(dir. Peter Wood; with Hordern as Moore and Julie Covington
as Dotty); Aldwych Th., 1 Apr. 1985 (dir. Peter Wood;

with Paul Eddington as Moore and Felicity Kendal as Dotty).
Published: London: Faber, 1972; revised ed., 1973 (with note
by Stoppard on the two 'most noticeable' changes. Stoppard
again 'adjusted' for the 1985 revival, making it 'more
appropriate' to the cast and to bring references up-to-date).

*The new Radical-Liberal Party has made the ex-Minister of Agri-
culture Archbishop of Canterbury, British astronauts are
scrapping with each other on the moon, and sprightly academics
steal about London by night indulging in murderous gymnastics:
this is the kind of manic, futuristic, topsy-turvy world in which
Tom Stoppard's dazzling new play,* Jumpers, *is lunatically set.
. . . Like most of Stoppard's work, the play is built around a
series of bizarre juxtapositions and the fundamental one here is
the marriage of an ageing moral philosopher [George Moore] to
an ex-musical comedy queen [Dotty]. In their television-
panelled house, he spends the day wrestling with a convoluted
lecture on God, the infinite, the nature of aesthetics, the concept
of good and evil: she meanwhile lounges in her bedroom lascivi-
ously entertaining her husband's university boss [Archie] and
watching the installation on the box of the new radical, ration-
alist government. On top of this Stoppard builds a spiralling
comedy of misunderstanding involving an Ortonian police
inspector [Bones] and the murder the previous night of a
gymnastic academic [McFee].*

Michael Billington, *The Guardian*, 3 Feb. 1972, p. 10

The conception of the play
[Interviewing Stoppard, Ronald Hayman remarked that *Jumpers*
seemed to take its starting point from the moment in *Rosencrantz and Guildenstern* when Rosencrantz says, 'Shouldn't we
be doing something constructive?' and Guildenstern asks him,
'What did you have in mind? A short blunt human pyramid?'] I
did begin with that image. Speaking as a playwright — which is a
category that must have its own boundary marks, because a
novelist couldn't say what I'm about to say — I thought: 'How
marvellous to have a pyramid of people on a stage, and a rifle
shot, and one member of the pyramid just being blown out of it
and the others imploding on the hole as he leaves'. I really like
theatrical events, and I was in a favourable position. Because of the

success of *Rosencrantz* it was on the cards that the National
Theatre would do what I wrote, if I didn't completely screw it
up, and it has forty, fifty actors on the pay-roll. You can actually
write a play for ten gymnasts. . . . It's perfectly true that having
shot this man out of the pyramid, and having him lying on the
floor, I didn't know who he was or who had shot him or why or
what to do with the body. . . . So one worked from a curiously
anti-literary starting point. . . . At the same time there's more
than one point of origin for a play, and the only useful metaphor
I can think of for the way I think I write my plays is conver-
gences of different threads. Perhaps carpet-making would suggest
something similar. One of the threads was the entirely visual
image of the pyramid of acrobats, but while thinking of that
pyramid I knew I wanted to write a play about a professor of
moral philosophy, and it's the work of a moment to think that
there was a metaphor at work in the play already between acrobatics, mental acrobatics, and so on. Actually it's not a bad way
of getting excited about a play.

Stoppard, interviewed by Ronald Hayman in
Tom Stoppard (London, 1977), p. 4-5

[*Jumpers* is] just the thought process of any intelligent person.
It could have been about a playwright or a vicar. In fact I should
have done it about a vicar and then you could have lost his
trousers in the third act. And the police could have come in. The
funniest line in the English theatre appears in a Ben Travers farce.
It is 'arrest several of these vicars'. The word 'several' is actually
the funniest word in the English language, but it has to be in context. The presentation [of *Jumpers*] guys, parodies and mimics
academic philosophy, which I got from reading books of that
kind in large numbers. Dons talk like they write. I read it with
great enjoyment, it was really very stimulating as well as absurd.
I have got very little desire to read any more of it now because
the entire operation seems to be taking place in a large plastic
bubble. . . . There were three or four claimants to the vacant title
for the original of George Moore, though there was no original.

Stoppard, quoted by Mark Amory, 'The Joke's the Thing',
Sunday Times Magazine, 9 June 1974, p. 72, 74

The 'central concern' of the play
[In the play, Moore says 'A remarkable number of apparently
intelligent people are baffled by the fact that a different group of

apparently intelligent people profess to a knowledge of God, when commonsense tells *them*, the first group of apparently intelligent people, that knowledge is only a possibility in matters that can be demonstrated to be true or false, such as that the Bristol train leaves from Paddington.'] I will tell you what was at the back of my mind in that speech. It is a fact that I know dozens of rational humanists who have a very hard-headed attitude to any mysticality in the theological tradition, and are very articulate and sceptical and scathing about it — *and read their horoscopes*. One does find that people accept horoscopes, not with any sort of firm conviction or absolute belief, but the very fact that horoscopes exist *at all* in a world which is said to be — at least in Western Europe — over sixty per cent non-churchgoing at best, suggests that everybody has a repository of a 'mystical' awareness that there is a lot more to them than meets the microscope. It's a difficult thing to express in terms which are not, if you like, 'spiritual' or 'mystical,' but I think that almost everybody would admit to having this sense that some things actually are better than others in a way which is not, in fact, rational. That, roughly, is the central concern of the play — *Jumpers*.

Stoppard, interviewed by Joseph McCullough in
Under Bow Bells (London: Sheldon Press, 1974), p. 163-4

On philosophy
[I began writing about an] abstract proposition — moral values are purely social conventions or, alternatively, they refer to some absolute divinity. . . . I think that Wittgenstein said that philosophy wasn't a subject, it was an activity. Most of the propositions I'm interested in have been kidnapped and dressed up by academic philosophy, but they are in fact the kind of propositions that would occur to any intelligent person in his bath. They're not academic questions, simply questions which have been given academic status. Philosophy can be reduced to a small number of questions which are battled about in most bars most nights. . . . I've always thought that the idea of God is absolutely preposterous, but slightly more plausible than the alternative proposition that, given enough time, some green slime could write Shakespeare's sonnets.

Stoppard, quoted by Mel Gussow, '*Jumpers* Author
Is Verbal Gymnast', *New York Times*, 23 Apr. 1974, p. 36

As much as anything, this is an anti-Skinner play. . . . Skinner is a highly provocative, fascinating, intelligent, brilliant wrong-headed oaf.

Mel Gussow, 'Stoppard Refutes Himself, Endlessly',
New York Times, 26 Apr. 1972, p. 54

When I first asked [Stoppard] what the play was about, [he] said, 'It's about a man trying to write a lecture'. But for me it was about a man trying to write a lecture *while his wife was stuck with a corpse in the next room.*

Peter Wood (director of first production), in programme
of the National Theatre revival, 1976

Michael Hordern on playing George Moore
Stoppard's a marvellous word-carpenter, but intricate, and I do find it difficult 'study'. I've got some very, very long speeches and I found it difficult to work my way through them. As with Bernard Shaw — not that I have got any time for that old bore — you can't paraphrase. If you get into difficulties you've had it, because it's such closely woven, closely tailored stuff. I have never read philosophy or studied philosophy, and the way a philosopher's brain works is foreign to me. And the way philosophers speak. Which makes this very difficult indeed to learn. I won't go as far as to say it's like learning in a foreign language, but indeed the words don't go in the direction that I personally would use if I wanted to say the same thing. One of the great points of the play is that this character talks philosophy. It's his character — he's the university don who talks philosophically, donnishly. But I find it difficult also to follow the intellectual progress of worrying away at a philosophical point and not letting it drop, going on and on, then seeing another little side-turning and going up that one, because you don't want to let the slightest little philosophical point drop or you won't prove your case and so on and the sentences get as long as that. But once you've got it, it's immensely enjoyable to play. Any play that has a strong sense of the ridiculous appeals to me, and of course Stoppard's work does.

Michael Hordern, in Ronald Hayman,
Playback 2 (London, 1973), p. 81

Paul Eddington on playing George Moore
George really has an awful lot to say, collecting his ideas for a

37

lecture. The first speech lasts about twenty minutes. And no cues are thrown at him. Ideally his thoughts flow in logical sequence, one following naturally upon another. But sometimes he gets his thoughts tangled up. . . . I'm not myself an oral philosopher like George. But I must say that if it's possible to enjoy learning, I'm enjoying this one. Usually it's real donkey work. . . . Essentially it's a discussion on the existence or otherwise of God. . . The funny side of George in *Jumpers* comes from the fact that he's a man with his head so totally in the clouds that he fails to see that his wife is being unfaithful to him.

Paul Eddington, quoted by Gordon Gow,
'Taking on *Jumpers*', *Plays*, Mar. 1985, p. 10

Diana Rigg on playing Dotty
I didn't understand it at first. Nobody did. Tom came over to see me and spent two hours making a path in the carpet telling me what it was all about. . . . Everything in this play is perfectly logical. Everything ties in, but it doesn't tie in the sequence that we, as theatre-people, are used to. More often than not the clue to the person's dilemma comes 35 minutes *before* the fact, which is a complete inversion of how it's normally done. Tom expects his audiences to lean forward in their seats and take note of absolutely everything because in order to understand the play it is necessary. If you miss the clues your enjoyment is halved.

Dottie was a student of Professor George Moore, then married him. She became a singing star in the genre of Anne Shelton or Dorothy Squire and sang ballads about the moon, 'Blue Moon', 'Shine on Harvest Moon', 'Moonlight in Vermont'. Then suddenly we landed an Englishman on the moon (it's that much in the future) and in consequence she had a breakdown. If you consider it, it's perfectly logical. Hitherto the moon has always been an unattainable thing. We've used it as a symbol of all our ideals. And suddenly a man is up there, looking down on us and seeing us as just 'an earth,' a very local thing. And the laws which we had believed were all-powerful and forever suddenly appeared in a different light. . . .

Both Dottie and George have an incredible selfishness about them. She is selfish about herself and her state. Which I think is realistic. People having, or who have had, a nervous breakdown are very concerned about themselves and how they feel, and also highly sensitive about other people's reactions to their condition.

Twice she appeals to George openly, and twice he's incapable of reaching her or giving her any comfort, because he simply doesn't understand. He's very logical. He plods along in his dogged fashion till he reaches a conclusion. She's much more mercurial. And when he's presented with these oblique emotional situations of hers, which have nothing to do with the conversation that they have been having up until that point, he's absolutely bewildered.

She has her breakdown, retires to her room, has him in from time to time to tease him, play with him, appeal to him. They're not actually having any sex. He says so. They don't really have much in common because there's also this creature Archie who's the Vice-Chancellor, *and* a psychiatrist *and* a few other things. He's representative of where her mind is at the moment, and he's her prop and stay. The audience aren't to know whether she and Archie are having an affair or not, but they're certainly very close. George suspects them, but won't do anything about it.

Diana Rigg, quoted by Margaret Tierney,
'Marriage Lines', *Plays and Players*, Mar. 1972, p. 26-7

On the National Theatre productions

[Hordern] finds the passion as well as the oddity in George; his attempts to articulate his faith are rather moving. Elsewhere he prepares his speech in a series of beaming spurts, taking brief self-hugging trips around the stage whenever inspiration strikes, rounding off his sentences with a triumphant nasal swoop — vocal italics — whenever he wishes, by pointing a contemporary metaphor to rout the forces of trendiness on their own ground. Leading these forces is Archie, vice-chancellor of George's university, for whom attempts to arrive at the roots of morality have little significance. Incidentally a man of means, he is primarily a man of ends, and ruthless in attaining them. His interests are wide; to please him, philosophers are athletes. George, of course, is out of step on both counts. George is a duffer, Archie is omni-competent, and the play foresees a government of Archies. (Though the spirit of the work is joyous and funny, its import is black.) Mr. Stoppard seems happier, though, with failure than success; I have seen two good actors play Archie (Graham Crowden last time, Julian Glover this) and they both came out wooden.

Robert Cushman, 'Moral Gymnastics',
The Observer, 26 Sept. 1976, p. 24

I found Peter Wood's revival rather less satisfying than his original production four-odd years ago. The trouble isn't so much the principal substitution, which is Julie Covington, earthier and more credibly distraught than Diana Rigg as George's chanteuse-wife, Dottie. It is that the general tone has become too manic, too frantic. Bernard Gallagher overplays the caricature detective, Bones, quite dreadfully, and even Michael Hordern, though still very fetching as George, is apt to exaggerate his mad-professor mannerisms. There is simply too much scratching, clearing of the throat, distracted wriggling of the shoulders and emphatic furrowing of the forehead.

> Benedict Nightingale, 'Not so Farce',
> *New Statesman*, 1 Oct. 1976, p. 457

On the worlds of the play
The play is a plea for ethical moorings in a world seemingly adrift on expediency. Dotty's breakdown is precipitated by Astronaut Scott's abandonment of Astronaut Oates on the dusty surface of the moon; and the power-seeking Archie, arch-Jumper of amoralism, emerges in the end as the most likely candidate for murderer of McFee, since the latter-day Scott's reversal of altruism may also have been the cause of the dead Jumper's intended apostasy. This is pure interpretative speculation, of course. . . . the zany, kaleidoscopic world they each inhabit makes it impossible to be sure who commited the crime — or, for that matter, if what has happened is a crime at all.

> R.P. Draper, 'Stoppard at Play',
> *Times Higher Education Supplement*, 14 Oct. 1983, p. 21

It would be unfair to Stoppard to suggest that the play exists on two different levels: Shavian debate and Drury Lane dazzle. For what is remarkable about him as a writer is the way he makes the imagery and the ideas interact. To take an obvious instance, the logical positivist who so spectacularly pops it in the first scene believes, so we learn, that murder is not inherently wrong. He is thereby both the victim of his own philosophy and the trigger of a very funny farce-plot in which his corpse swings listlessly from a cupboard door.

> Michael Billington, '*Jumpers*', *The Guardian*,
> 23 Oct. 1976

Stoppard's problem is, first of all, that he is himself the arche-

typal jumper, always in mid-*salto mortale* between metaphysical
puns and absurdist metaphors: swinging brilliantly from an
epigram, but fatally neglecting the safety network of solid character, plot, and structure to protect his neck. George and Dotty
interest us, but Stoppard tells us far too little about them, seldom
even letting them inhabit the same side of the stage. . . . The
roles, regrettably, remain divided into jumping and non-jumping
ones, and the play's basic concept fails to coalesce. Subjects pro-
liferate profligately: philosophy, religion, politics, love, the
survival of mankind, psychiatry, linguistics, the music hall . . . and
its influence on culture – even the acting out of the paradoxes of
Zeno. The stage cannot cope with all this: it is a muscle-bound
Achilles vainly lumbering after Stoppard's tortuous tortoise. And
there is even something arrogant about trying to convert the
history of Western culture into a series of blackout sketches,
which is very nearly what *Jumpers* is up to.

John Simon, 'Flying Philosophers, Poetic Pederasts',
New York, 11 Mar. 1974, p. 84

The play is concerned with the existence of God and the definition of goodness; both of which, Stoppard implies, have been
brought further into doubt by space exploration. For once he has
included a key speech, forecasting the spread of moral anarchy
from our provincial position in the universe: 'truths taken on
trust never had such edges before'. That line comes from Miss
Rigg in the person of a retired musical comedy star married to a
professor of philosophy; from which you may gather that this is
a marriage of dramatic convenience. It is Stoppard's way to start
with an idea and work outwards to the characters: the idea in this
case being the relationship between flesh and intellect. But given
the abstraction of their origin, they do achieve as much personal
reality as the action requires.

Irving Wardle, *'Jumpers'*, *The Times*, 3 Feb. 1972, p. 13

This is the attack, not so much of a right-wing dramatist upon
leftist extremism, rather of a principled writer upon a society
whose standards seem to him increasingly pragmatic, expedient,
amoral. . . . *Jumpers* is a courageous attempt to move beyond the
social criticism that mainly preoccupies the contemporary theatre
into a realm of metaphysics almost entirely ignored by it, to
relate the two, and, doing so, to raise issues of rare size and
import; and this is achieved, not only with a theatrical extrava-

gance that verges on the outrageous, but with a nice sense of individual character.

Benedict Nightingale, An Introduction to Fifty Modern British Plays (London, 1982), p. 418, 422

A selection of other articles and reviews

Jonathan Bennett, 'Philosophy and Mr. Stoppard', *Philosophy,* L (1975), p. 5-18.

Tim Brassell, '*Jumpers*: a Happy Marriage?', *Gambit*, No. 37 (Summer 1981), p. 43-59.

G.B. Crump, 'The Universe as Murder Mystery: Tom Stoppard's *Jumpers*', *Contemporary Literature*, XX (1979), p. 354-68.

Mary R. Davidson, 'Historical Homonyms: a New Way of Naming in Tom Stoppard's *Jumpers*', *Modern Drama*, XXII (1979), p. 305-13.

Paul Delaney, 'The Flesh and the Word in *Jumpers*', *Modern Language Quarterly*, XLII (1981), p. 369-88.

Weldon B. Durham, 'Symbolic Action in Tom Stoppard's *Jumpers, Theatre Journal*, XXXII (1980), p. 169-79.

Lucina P. Gabbard, 'Stoppard's *Jumpers*: a Mystery Play', *Modern Drama*, XX (1977), p. 87-95.

Michael Hinden, '*Jumpers:* Stoppard and the Theater of Exhaustion', *Twentieth Century Literature*, XXVII (1981), p. 1-15.

James Morwood, '*Jumpers* Revisited', *Agenda*, XVIII-XIX (1981), p. 135-41.

Artist Descending a Staircase

Play for radio.
Transmitted: BBC Radio 3, 14 Nov. 1972 (dir. John Tydeman).
Published: with *Where Are They Now?* (London: Faber, 1973); and in *Four Plays for Radio* (1984).

Our old friend Tape Recorder appeared at the start, with a recording of the last seconds in the life of Donner, an old painter. Donner shares a flat at the top of a flight of stairs with Martello, an old sculptor, and Beauchamp, an old tape recorder buff. He is heard to say, 'Ah, there you are' before he falls to his death screaming.

Which of the other two did it? Does it matter? Not really, since what we are doing is coasting about in time, listening to the three artists comment, explicitly and implicitly, fluent with epigrams, on another old friend, Reality. Their relationship long ago with a blind girl called Sophie, who killed herself by jumping through a window, is what they all cling to. Martello (Stephen Murray) has carved her out of sugar. Donner (Carleton Hobbs) was painting her before he fell downstairs.

Back we go to Paris and the day she died, then back to the day they first met her, then back to a time before they knew her – a stylized but beautifully comic account of a holiday in France in August 1914. Now the play unwinds in the reverse direction – the day of the first meeting, followed by the day she died, followed by the present again. This was as ingenious as poems whose first and last lines rhyme, and so on until the rhymes meet in the middle. It was altogether a marvellous play for those who like ingenuity; less marvellous for those who prefer the mechanism out of sight.

The ending was suitably uncertain. Sophie, we learn, had chosen Beauchamp (Rolf Lefebvre) as her lover because before she went totally blind she fancied one of the three as he stood in front of a particular painting, and later worked out that it must have been Beauchamp. But Martello (fifty years later) tells Donner she probably mixed up the paintings, which means it was Donner she fancied. Since he has been eating his heart out ever since, perhaps he jumped, too, poor chap.

Paul Ferris, 'Tempting Carrot',
The Observer, 19 Nov. 1972, p. 37

[*Artist Descending*] was like a dry run, in a sort of way [for *Travesties*]. It was two bites at the same apple. Sometimes the same bite at the same apple, actually.

Stoppard, interviewed by Nancy Shields Hardin,
Contemporary Literature, XXII (Spring 1981), p. 156

I want to read a few lines from your plays and to recall some things you said to me in the past, to see if you still believe them. Here's a line from Artist Descending a Staircase: *'Skill without imagination is craftsmanship and gives us many useful objects such as wickerwork picnic baskets. Imagination without skill gives us modern art.'*

Stoppard: I believe that.

Which is more important, imagination or skill?

Stoppard: Imagination, because it fulfils your internal life. If you're making a living at it, you'd better have some skill.

Another line from that play: 'How can one justify a work of art to a man with an empty belly?' Your answer was, 'Make it edible'.

Stoppard: That's not an entirely adequate answer, is it? Somebody's on the ropes there. As a matter of fact, I don't think art needs that sort of justification. You can't wait until everybody is fed before you begin art. What happens is that they're hungry and they're starved for art.

Mel Gussow, 'Play on Words',
New York Times, 1 Jan. 1984, Sec. VI, p. 18

Travesties

Play in two acts.
First London Production: Aldwych Th., 10 June 1974 (dir. Peter Wood; with John Wood as Carr).
First New York production: Ethel Barrymore Th., 30 Oct. 1975 (dir. Peter Wood; with John Wood as Carr).
Published: London: Faber, 1975. (A speech by Joyce, cut from the text, was published as 'Leftover from *Travesties'* in *Adam*, Nos. 431-433 (1980), p. 11-12. Philip Gaskell's book, *From Writer to Reader: Studies in Editorial Method* (Oxford, 1978), includes a unique study (p. 245-62) comparing the script, published text, and tape-recordings of performance of this play, showing that the three differ considerably, and concluding that it is difficult to decide which should be seen as the true text.)

The play starts with Henry Carr as an old man reminiscing about his time in the British consulate in Zurich during World War I, which leads into a (faulty) re-creation of his memories. Carr was a real figure, but known only through biographies of James Joyce: Carr sued Joyce for the price of the pair of trousers Carr bought to wear in Joyce's production of Wildes's The Importance of Being Earnest. *The play builds around the coincidence that Lenin and the Dadaist Tristan Tzara were in Zurich at the same time. They also take on identities in Wilde's play, Joyce as Lady Bracknell, Lenin as Miss Prism, and Tzara as John Worthing: Cecily and Gwendolyn also appear from* The Importance. *Stoppard's introduction and acknowledgements to the text cite 11 books used as sources, also revealing that he received a letter from Henry Carr's widow.*

Travesties is a work of fiction which makes use, and misuse, of history. Scenes which are self-evidently documentary mingle with others which are just as evidently fantastical. People who were hardly aware of each other's existence are made to collide; real people and imaginary people are brought together without ceremony; and events which took place months, and even years, apart are presented as synchronous. For the luxury of such liberties I am indebted to writers who allowed themselves none. . . . History rather than imagination places Lenin, Joyce, and the Dadaist Tristan Tzara in Zurich at one and the same time. History, too, offers us one short conversation between Lenin and a Dadaist, recounted in the Motherwell book [*The Dada Painters and Poets*], and also the possibility of a meeting between Lenin and Joyce (though it is hard to imagine what they would have to say to each other). But for the most part *Travesties* is presented through the fevered imagination of its principal character [Carr].

Stoppard, programme note to first London production

Initial thinking on the play
It might be nice to do a two-act thing, with one act a Dadaist play on Communist ideology and the other an ideological functional drama about Dadaists.

Stoppard, quoted in Mel Gussow, 'Stoppard Refutes Himself, Endlessly', *New York Times*, 26 Apr. 1972, p. 54

When I start writing I find it difficult, except on simple questions, to know where I stand — even in *Travesties* in the argument on art between James Joyce and Tristran Tzara. Temperamentally and intellectually, I'm very much on Joyce's side, but I found it persuasive to write Tzara's speech.

Stoppard, quoted in Mel Gussow, 'Stoppard's Intellectual Cartwheels Now with Music', *New York Times*, 29 July 1979, Sec. II, p. 1, 22

[*Travesties*] asks whether the words 'revolutionary' and 'artist' are capable of being synonymous, or whether they are mutually exclusive, or something in between.

Stoppard, 'Ambushes for the Audience', p. 11

One of the impulses in *Travesties* is to try to sort out what my answer would in the end be if I was given enough time to think every time I'm asked why my plays aren't political, or ought they to be? . . .

How did you arrive at the idea of making the scheme accommodate Tristan Tzara in the role of John Worthing?

It was a combination of joke for joke's sake and playwright's convenience. Obviously I'd already realized that I wanted to use the *Importance* scheme, and at the same time Tzara was a Romanian. I can't bear the thought of an actor doing a Maurice Chevalier accent. I can't bear Maurice Chevalier. Therefore one must say, 'All right, in that case it's going to be done in perfect English, and therefore I'll put in a previous scene in which he has a French-Romanian accent and he's monocled and ludicrous and outrageous, just to establish that'. One of the things that tickled me about the situation is that it's rather like one of those Magritte paintings in which there's a picture of a shoe, and underneath it's labelled 'A HORSE'. I think it's the same sort of joke when you're faced with the image of John Hurt with his perfect, eternal English languor sitting there, and someone saying to him, 'You bloody Romanian wog!' It's Magritte labelling, and I can't think off-hand of any more dignified intellectual credential for that aspect of the play. . . .

What about Cecily's lecture at the beginning of Act Two? Surely you're not expecting the audience to digest so much information so quickly?

There are several levels going here, and one of them is that what I personally like is the theatre of audacity. I thought, 'Right. We'll have a rollicking first act, and they'll all come back from their gin-and-tonics thinking "Isn't it fun? What a lot of lovely jokes!" And they'll sit down, and this pretty girl will start talking about the theory of Marxism and the theory of capitalism and the theory of value. And the smiles, because they're not prepared for it, will atrophy.' And that to me was like a joke in itself. But the important thing was that I'd ended the first act with what at that stage was a lengthy exposition of Dada. I wanted to begin the second with a corresponding exposition of how Lenin got to Zurich. . . . What's altered is the sympathy level you have with Lenin. When you read the words on the page there's a sense in which Lenin keeps convicting himself out of his own mouth. It's absurd. It's full of incredible syllogisms. All the publishing and libraries and bookshops and newspapers must be controlled by the Party. The press will be free.

Jumpers and *Travesties* are very similar plays. No one's said that, but they're so similar that were I to do it a third time it would be a bore. You start with a prologue which is slightly strange. Then you have an interminable monologue which is rather funny. Then you have scenes. Then you end up with another monologue. And you have unexpected bits of music and dance, and at the same time people are playing ping-pong with various intellectual arguments.

Stoppard, interviewed by Ronald Hayman, in
Tom Stoppard, p. 2, 3-4, 9-10, 12

With Henry Carr . . . we discussed many possible ways of achieving the change from age to youth. . . . I favoured a more simple, emblematic device. The change of age is actually done by a change of hat: nothing more. When I come on, the dressing-gown says very old and the panama hat says uprooted English emigré probably living abroad because the gin is cheaper. I didn't want to do a pyrotechnic thing that drew attention to itself. I wanted to keep the background clear because in Tom's play the word is all. The word is beating back the silence, beating back the darkness. Thought is all we've got, says Tom, otherwise the dark, the jungle, will close in on us. I think this is what makes his plays so moving and even tragic.

John Wood, interviewed by Michael Billington,
'Medium of the Moment', *The Guardian*, 11 Aug. 1975

[Hugh Hebert also gives an interesting description of *Travesties* in rehearsal in 'Domes of Zurich', *The Guardian*, 7 June 1974, p. 10]

Travesties has a certain resemblance to Nabokov's *Pale Fire* in
that it's narrated by an extraordinary, erratic old gentleman who
has (a) a poor memory, (b) powerful reactionary prejudices and
(c) a high sense of fantasy. As Tom puts it, the story is like a toy
train that occasionally jumps the rails and has to be restarted at
the point where it goes wild. It's a view of history seen prismat-
ically through the view of Henry Carr. At one point Tom was
thinking of calling it *Prism*. . . . The play was written for John
Wood. There aren't many young actors with the farce body and
the Shakespearian labial facility and the sincerity and the energy.

Peter Wood, interviewed by Ronald Hayman,
The Times, 8 June 1974, p. 9

I find it difficult to write in calm, measured tones about Tom
Stoppard's *Travesties*: a dazzling pyrotechnical feat that
combines Wildean pastiche, political history, artistic debate,
spoof-reminiscence, and song-and-dance in marvellously judicious
proportions. The text itself is a dense Joycean web of literary
allusions, yet it also radiates sheer intellectual *joie de vivre*.

Michael Billington, *'Travesties'*, *The Guardian*,
11 June 1974

Wood gives several brilliant performances as Carr. There is the
young consul basking in Swiss neutrality ('the entente cordiality
of it'); the blushing amateur actor, seduced by appeals to the
memory of his brilliant Goneril at Eton into essaying the part of
Algernon (though he looks, to be truthful, as though his name
were Ernest); and, when his memories are done, the final unwilling
return to old age, his hands and feet still obstinately going through
the motions of a swaying, decelerating foxtrot, as the grin of
youth fades from his face.

Robert Cushman, 'Stoppard Run Wilde',
The Observer, 16 June 1974, p. 31

. . . another Stoppard study in human irrelevance. Like Rosencrantz and Guildenstern, like George, the professor in *Jumpers*,
Carr is a pooh-stick in the River of Fate, swirled to and fro by
currents, not recognizing the bridges under which he slowly
drifts. After three or four plays, this harping on irrelevance seems
irrelevant in itself. Is Stoppard suggesting that men are always
adrift, in which case he could have selected a more startling pooh-

stick, such as Lenin? Or is he simply pointing out that, from different angles, history changes colour and shape, a familiar point but one which, in a world full of dogmas, is worth stressing? My view is that Stoppard merely uses this theme of irrelevance as a pad from which to launch a variety of literary pastiches, the chief being that of Wilde's play, but with a cluster of secondary ones, such as Joycean limericks and Dadaistic poems which prove accidentally to have more sense than their originals. . . . A genteel boredom creeps in, a yawn of pleasure.

> John Elsom, 'Pooh-sticks',
> *The Listener*, 20 June 1974, p. 801

I don't think the extravaganza quite comes off as an autonomous creation. For instance, the character of Joyce is a failure, a sort of blank, because it is easier to show how non-art is silly and political dogmatism limited than it is to explain how good art comes to be good.

> John Weightman, 'Art versus Life',
> *Encounter*, XLIII (Sept. 1974), p. 59

Under the sheen of its immense daring, the play reveals a touching centre, a study of a useless but endearing chap frantically beating off the onrush of obscurity. His struggle is inept, but ineptitude has been his life companion. His hilarious attempts to spy on Lenin in Zurich, whence the Russian leader had already fled, are achingly funny. No less so are Carr's pathetic stabs at coping with intellectual life. 'I don't know it', he says of Wilde's play, 'but I've heard of it and I don't like it'. That philistine manifesto resounds through later scenes like a litany.

> Alan Rich, 'Memorabilia',
> *New York*, 17 Nov. 1975, p. 102

There are really three plays, as well as four diverse personalities, in *Travesties*. First there is Carr's *A la recherche du temps perdu*, his little syntactical trot down memory lane, his unctuous refamiliarizing with the great. Here the attitude-striking has substance and consistency, and it forms an outer shell or casing, beginning and ending the play. There is sentiment here, time, character, nostalgia: these parts, short though they are, are the best in the play.

Secondly, there is the Wildean send-up, with Henry, Cecily

(prettily and loquaciously played by Beth Morris) and Gwendolen pirouetting among the drawing-room persiflage of Tzara and Joyce. Clever, all this stuff, and occasionally very funny indeed: full of acrostics, limericks, parody, absurdity; quite exhilarating: altogether a relief to be teased and dazzled by words for once.

Thirdly, there is the Lenin thread, the grafting of political reality on to the essential frivolity of the dadaists, or the 'Our Father in Art' Joyce.

Garry O'Connor, *'Travesties'*, *Plays and Players*,
July 1974, p. 34

Stoppard's work has always been particularly interesting because of the way in which he explores the asethetic problems of the representation of reality. In this play it isn't only the fact that we watch a writer's imaginative resurrection of three men in history, making them meet and talk in a way they never did, but also that within the play particular episodes are played back, as in a film sequence, a number of times. This becomes both a device to provide us with information (on the progress of the twentieth century history up to 1917) but also to show us that at each and every point a writer makes choices about what to say and how to say it. Stoppard's licence in his version of 'history' is a salutary reminder to look closely at other apparently truthful glimpses into the past via personal reminiscence.

Michelene Wandor, *'Travesties'*, *Spare Rib*,
No. 38 (Aug. 1975), p. 42

The play is a very deliberate and profound attack on socialist theories of art, is itself a strong blow for the unfashionable 'art for the sake of art.' . . . He seems to me to be saying, more fully than in *Jumpers*, but it was there too, be socialist by all means or even especially, but don't think that the theory must explain everything – particularly art, which is the very badge of freedom and spontaneity among men and women; for if you think that it must, when it so plainly doesn't, then you end up coercing people to fit the facts. . . . The more you seek to advance the more you need to discriminate, have piss, pushpin, and poetry by all means, only 'God send that you don't make them in the same hat'. *Ulysses* is humanity vindicated. And all this is in the structure of the play even before Lenin speaks at length. . . . [Stoppard] attacks the Leninist theory of art with like gusto, seeming madness, jolly obscenity, frantic word play, punishing puns, and incredible imaginative and irrelevant invention of plots all exemplary of how free we all could be just by trying.

Bernard Crick, *'Travesties'*,
Times Higher Education Supplement, 2 Aug. 1974, p. 13

A selection of other articles and reviews
Carol Billman, 'The Art of History in Tom Stoppard's *Travesties'*, *Kansas Quarterly*, XII, 4 (Fall 1980), p. 47-52.
John William Cooke, 'The Optical Allusion', *Modern Drama*, XXIV (Dec. 1981), p. 525-39.
Margaret Gold, 'Who Are the Dadas of *Travesties?*', *Modern Drama*, XXI (Mar. 1978), p. 59-66.
David K. Rod, 'Carr's Views on Art and Politics in Tom Stoppard's *Travesties'*, *Modern Drama*, XXVI (Dec. 1983), p. 536-42.

The Boundary

Play for television, written with Clive Exton.
Transmitted: 'Eleventh Hour', BBC-1, 19 July 1975 (dir.
Mike Newell).
Unpublished.

Two lexicographers, trapped in their verbiage (as though belonging to their big-brother of a play, Jumpers*), find their files blown all over their gothicky work-room. Under the paper lies Brenda, wife of the one, mistress of the other, and presumably dead. She comes to, cracks a few malapropisms, and is conked on the head again by the villain of the piece, a cricket-ball through the window.*

David Pryce-Jones, 'Lawrentian Models',
The Listener, 24 July 1975, p. 117

[The 'Eleventh Hour' series was of plays conceived and written in one week, transmitted live, in the hope of both topicality and extra tension. In an *Omnibus* TV programme about it (21 Sept. 1975), Stoppard and Exton said that they saw it only as an elaborate party game, with collaboration making personal statements impossible.]

The play's devices mostly seemed to reflect Stoppard's well-known obsessions: the don with the flighty wife (*Jumpers*), the bizarre stage-picture which the action clarifies (*After Magritte*), the body on the floor (*The Real Inspector Hound*). Stoppard never minds using an idea a second time so long as the plot redefines it. And once again the plot was a honey, with the whole chain of events remaining unintelligible until a few minutes before the end, when a cricket ball flying through the window shook everything into shape. The lexical bravura ranged from parfor-the-course Mrs. Malaprop ('enough of this virago!') to vaulting inspiration ('macaroni' was a short American actor).

Clive James, *The Observer*, 27 July 1975, p. 22

Dirty Linen

Play in one act, incorporating the short play, *New-Found-Land*.
First production: Ambiance Lunch-Hour Th. Club at Almost
    Free Th., London, 6 Apr. 1976 (dir. Ed Berman); trans. to
    Arts Th., 16 June 1976.
First New York production: Golden Th., 11 Jan. 1977
    (dir. Ed Berman).
Published: London: Faber, 1976.

Dirty Linen is a hilarious diversion, being set in the House of Commons where a select committee is investigating the sexual conduct of MPs. The moral standards of 192 of them have been called into question since they have been seen in compromising company in various nightspots, mostly as fate would have it, at the Coq d'Or. . . . Let us observe Mr. Stoppard as he deftly sets the scene, with Cocklebury-Smythe MP and Mr. McTeazle MP (both [Conservative], presumably) exchanging French tags with wolfish politeness and battling with pieces of female underwear which keep inexplicably emerging from their briefcases. Edward de Souza and Benjamin Whitrow play this passage with savage precision, and they are joined by Chamberlain, a breezy young bounder in a flash suit (Malcolm Ingram), the Chairman, Withenshaw, a Lancashire bulldozer with a nice line in masterful bonhomie (Peter Bowles), and French (Richard O'Callaghan), a fire-spitting prig who proves an unexpected catalyst. With this play Mr. Stoppard emerges as a social satirist. Gogol would smile with approval if he could see him animating these marvellously observed marionettes. It's a battlefield: we behold panic-stricken respectability besieged by panic-stricken sexuality. And throughout Mr. Stoppard keeps a watchful eye on the quirks of the committee-room, on the insolence and impotence of office, and on the irresistible oddities of character. . . . The American connection . . . takes the form of *New-Found-Land*, a playlet inserted, so to speak, into *Dirty Linen* and dealing with the application for British citizenship of a bearded American theatre director whose similarity to Ed Berman, director of the Almost Free and of the play, is probably coincidental.

John Peter, 'Members Only,' *Sunday Times*,
18 Apr. 1976, p. 37

Dirty Linen works nicely. But I don't think anybody would pretend it was naturalistic. In fact I had a very sweet letter from the Clerks' Department of the House of Commons, inviting me for a drink and pointing out certain discrepancies between the play and the reality it purports to present. *Dirty Linen* is as unlike *The Linden Tree* [by J.B. Priestley] in some ways as it is unlike Ionesco. . . . I had no interest in writing about the House of Commons actually. I wouldn't have written the play at all but for the necessity to fulfil a promise [to Berman for a play for his season marking the bicentenary of American independence]. *Dirty Linen* is a play in which a sexy dumb blonde walks on and is utterly patronized, and the play ends with the entire committee adopting the resolution which she said they ought to adopt on page four or whatever it is. She actually is Miss Common Sense rather than Miss Empty Head. Probably she wasn't properly established before she begins to show other sides to herself, but certainly the idea is that she's anybody's plaything, totally empty-headed, with a big bust, and occasionally makes comments which are disquietingly irrefutable, and ends up by controlling the whole committee. If one did the play again it would probably take three acts and be a Major Work, but to hell with that.

Stoppard, 'Second Interview', in Ronald Hayman,
Tom Stoppard, p. 137, 141

I thought of a high-powered commission, investigating something or other. Albert Einstein and an archbishop would be on the commission. There would be a staggering blonde who corrected the archbishop on theology and Einstein on physics. Then the commission turned into a special committee of Parliament. . . . If it were a movie, it would have to be made by the Boulting brothers, not Roman Polanski.

> Stoppard, quoted by John Leonard, 'Tom Stoppard Tries on a "Knickers Farce",' *New York Times*, 9 Jan. 1977, Sec. II, p. 1.

It is, like *The Real Inspector Hound*, just good, clean — or not-so-good and not-so-clean — fun with very simple concepts, pleasantly painted puppet characters, and occasionally quite sophisticated verbal structures.

> John Simon, 'Theatre Chronicle', *Hudson Review*, XXX (1977), p. 260.

Every Good Boy Deserves Favour

'A play for actors and orchestra.'

First performance: Royal Festival Hall, 1 July 1977, with the London Symphony Orchestra (dir. Trevor Nunn; with John Wood as Ivanov and Ian McKellen as Alexander).

First American production: Kennedy Centre, Washington, July 1978, with the Pittsburgh Symphony Orchestra (with John Wood as Ivanov and Eli Wallach as Alexander).

First New York production: Metropolitan Opera House, 30 July 1979.

Revived: Mermaid Th., London, 14 June 1978, with a chamber orchestra (dir. Trevor Nunn; with Ian McDiarmid as Ivanov and John Woodvine as Alexander); Barbican Centre, London, 25 June 1982, with the LSO (dir. Trevor Nunn; with David Suchet as Ivanov and Ian McKellen as Alexander).

Published: with *Professional Foul* (London: Faber, 1978).

Record: RCA, 1978 (with Ian Richardson as Ivanov and Ian McKellen as Alexander).

[The short scenes] are concerned with two inmates of a Soviet mental asylum. One is there because he thinks he owns an orchestra, the other because he has dared to write to Pravda *pointing out that some of his friends seem to have been locked up for reasons not wholly or indeed fractionally concerned with criminality or insanity. Both men are attended by a doctor who happens to play in a real orchestra, and the only three others we meet are the dissident's son, his strict party-line teacher and a*

comic-opera [colonel] who arrives at the last possible moment to release both inmates, not because of a change of Soviet heart but because of a confusion over their respective identities.

Sheridan Morley, *Shooting Stars*, p. 136

[In his 'Introduction', Stoppard explains how André Previn commissioned him 'to write something which had the need of a live full-size orchestra on stage', and how his ignorance of music and his lack of a subject prevented progress until he met Victor Fainberg, a Russian dissident who had been put in a mental hospital for political protest and had written about this in *Index*. 'My friend C' in the play is Vladimir Bukovsky, another dissident released as a result of Western protests in 1976. When Bukovsky attended a rehearsal, Stoppard and the actors were embarrassed by the juxtaposition of art and real-life suffering. Stoppard adds in an interview: 'One would have felt the same thing if *King Lear* had been based on fact and Gloucester had wandered in' ('Trad Tom Pops in', *Gambit*, No. 37 (1981), p. 7).]

It's not quite clear in the first version whether the colonel's mixed-up questioning is deliberate or not, whereas there's no doubt about that at all in the second version.

Stoppard: The actual text is identical. . . . It is supposed that the colonel knew exactly what he was doing, but it was only given one performance in the Royal Festival Hall, there was no second performance, and it was apparent that a lot of people misunderstood the way that the last scene was played: they thought the colonel had made a mistake. So when we came to the Mermaid Theatre we simply, as it were, acted it differently to make sure that it was understood that the colonel understood what he was doing. . . .

The play is written for severe physical limitations: three platforms about the size of this desk, one chair, one table, and the equation which makes the theatrical event rich enough would fail completely without the orchestra. It's really very simplified as a piece of playwriting, because it had to be quite short, you couldn't have any setting and you couldn't have any movement.

Stoppard, interviewed by Joost Kuurman,
Dutch Quarterly Review, X (1980), p. 53-4

Every Good Boy is an exercise, a clever answer to the technical problem posed by the original scheme. With all its sincere and deeply serious intentions, it only toys with its subject. It is not that the fate of the dissidents is too grave a theme for humour. Ridicule is a shrewd weapon to use against tyranny, as well as a force for courage and sanity in the user. But Stoppard has allowed himself to be carried away by his own comic invention. The triangle-player runs such zany riot in the opening scene that the play is caught in his clutches and the theme half smothered in its counterpoint. Farce and 'most ingenious paradox' once admitted, will not be dislodged, not even by the dissident's chilling account of his 'treatment', by drugs and torture, in a Moscow psychiatric clinic. Perhaps if Previn's accomplished, anonymous score had provided something more positive than background music and interludes for reflection, the drama's tragic ironies would have struck home; but I doubt it, given the emphasis of Stoppard's writing.

David Cairns, *Sunday Times*, 27 June 1982, p. 39

The confining of the two men in the same cell (or 'ward') seems to be the whim of the authors rather than of their jailers. It lacks the inevitability of the philosopher-gymnast equation in *Jumpers*. (The philosopher-footballer tie-up in *Professional Foul* falls somewhere between the two). . . . Ivanov's encounters with the psychiatrist who will declare him sane if he admits to madness recall *Catch-22*; but it is probably impossible to write comprehensively of the modern world without doing that. . . . The ending is majestic. . . . To the pleasure of seeing authority hoist with its own petard (and a hopeful comment on totalitarian stupidity) is added the satisfaction of poetic justice — but the music tells us that it is *only* poetic. It is not how things usually happen. This has all the irony of the *Threepenny Opera* finale. . . If a playwright wishes to fire us against injustice or the waste of life he must first convince us, in the quality of his own work, that life is worth living anyway. Mr. Stoppard's gaiety is a moral quality in itself.

Robert Cushman, 'Drama for Actors and Orchestra',
Observer, 18 June 1978, p. 26

How do you laugh at evil? What jest is fitting for a charnel-house? Where is the comedian who would begin his patter 'I say, I say, a funny thing happened to me on the way to Hell'? If you think these questions have no answers, you do not know Mr. Stoppard, whose *content* is the incarceration in Soviet madhouses of sane dissidents, but whose *form* nevertheless is a fiery comet of wit, of verbal felicities, of the most delicate irony and the ripest comic misunderstanding. . . . 'Rage, rage against the dying of the light'; gradually, as the huge, faultlessly-paced crescendo of Mr. Stoppard's play moves to its climax (itself a joke worthy of Voltaire), his *saeva indignatio*, still holding laughter by the hand, cuts deeper and deeper weals on the body of the wickedness he depicts. Yet although this is a profoundly moral work, the argument still undergoes the full transmutation of art, and is thereby utterly changed; as we emerged it was the fire and glitter of the play that possessed us, while its eternal truth, which is that the gates of hell shall not prevail, was by then inextricably embedded in our hearts.

Bernard Levin, 'Stoppard's Political Asylum',
Sunday Times, 3 July 1977, p. 37

Professional Foul

Play for television, written for Amnesty International's
Prisoner of Conscience Year.
Transmitted: 'Play of the Week', BBC-2, 24 Sept. 1977
(dir. Michael Lindsay-Hogg; with Peter Barkworth as
Anderson).
Published: with *Every Good Boy Deserves Favour* (London:
Faber, 1978); and with *Squaring the Circle* and *Every Good
Boy* (London: Faber, 1984).

*The framework is that of a thriller, with intermittent patches of
comedy. A Cambridge professor of ethics, on an academic visit
to Prague, gets caught up in the backwash of Charter 77's
struggle. A missed football match, an accidental scrape with the
secret police, and a sudden revelation of their methods in action
all help to precipitate a change in the hero, who discards the
sophisticated twaddle he had planned to present at his sympo-
sium. Instead, to the consternation of his hosts, he presents a
passionate declaration about the moral nature of human rights. . .
Everything hinged about the impact of wordless human suffering
on articulate spiritual atrophy, but the subsoil was rich in related
encounters — youth and age, courage and cowardice, sex and the*

*cerebrum, philosophy noble and debased. The yob ethics of foot-
ball threaded their punning way through far more of the play
than just those sections which dealt with the game itself.*
Michael Church, 'Starting with a Bang',
The Times, 29 Sept. 1977, p. 11

Professional Foul had to be realistic. . . . because whether the
audience is aware of it or not, and on the whole they aren't,
the effectiveness of dangerous theatrical devices on the stage
depends on them being difficult to do in the physical situation
you are working in. Once you have a camera and editing facilities,
I lose all interest in trying to astonish people by what actually
happens, because anything *can*.
Stoppard, quoted by Hugh Hebert, in 'A Playwright in Undis-
covered Country', *The Guardian*, 7 July 1979, p. 10

Professional Foul and *Jumpers* can each be described as a play
about a moral philosopher preoccupied with the true nature of
absolute morality, trying to separate absolute values from local
ones and local situations. That description would apply to either
play, yet one is a rampant farce and the other is a piece of naturalistic TV drama. . . . What happens is that [Anderson]'s got a
perfectly respectable philosophical thesis and he encounters a
mother and a child who are victims of this society, and it cuts
through all the theory. It's as though there are two moralities:
one to do with systems of government and an alternative morality to do with relationships between individuals. The latter
is governed by instinctive feelings about what good and bad
behaviour consist of and an instant and instinctive recognition of
each when they occur. The pay-off really is that when Anderson
puts his friend at risk by hiding the essay which he is smuggling
in his colleague's briefcase, he says something like, 'I thought you
would approve'! This is the man's public stance. And of course
his colleague makes the same discovery that it's all very well in
the bloody textbooks, but this is *me*, I could be in that jail, this
is *my* briefcase, you bastard! So it's more to do with a man being
educated by experience beyond the education he's received from
thinking. . . .

The reason why Anderson talks the way he does is because
people like him do talk like that. I can honestly say that I have
held Anderson's final view on the subject for years and years, and
years before Anderson ever existed. . . .

I wanted to write about somebody coming from England to a totalitarian society, brushing up against it, and getting a little soiled and a little wiser. I spent a long time wondering what to do . . . and I thought: a ballroom dancing team, with those wonderful ladies in tangerine tulle . . . 'Come Dancing in Prague' . . . but I was really interested in the moral implications, and the equation just simplified itself until the formation dancers became moral philosophers.

What you've got then is a desire to write about a moral philosopher who goes to Prague. An appeal is made to him by a former student, the appeal is rejected, he gets his nose rubbed in it slightly, learns, and acts. But what he learns isn't something which the writer is simultaneously learning in the course of writing the play. On the contrary, that's the end objective of the original desire to write the play.

> Stoppard, 'Trad Tom Pops in',
> *Gambit*, No. 37 (1981), p. 7-10

I'm as Czech as Czech can be. So you can see that with my desire to write something about human rights, the combination of my birth, my trips to Russia, my interest in Havel and his arrest, the appearance of Charter 77 were the linking threads that gave me the idea for *Professional Foul*.

> Stoppard, quoted by Milton Shulman, 'The Politicizing of
> Tom Stoppard', *New York Times*,
> 23 Apr. 1978, Sec. II, p. 3

Not all the footballing parallels work, but no other playwright could have found so apt an image for a calculated breaking of rules and then have devised so many reflections of it within the action of the play. Just about everyone in the play commits a professional foul at some point, and we are made to judge means and end in every case. There is one scene — the hero's encounter with his imprisoned student's wife and son — that goes deeper emotionally than anything he has written before.

> Robert Cushman, 'Nights of Opera and Telly',
> *Observer*, 2 Oct. 1977, p. 28

A selection of articles
Richard J. Buhr, 'Epistemology and Ethics in Tom Stoppard's *Professional Foul*', *Comparative Drama*, XII (Winter 1979-

80), p. 320-9.

Richard J. Buhr, 'The Philosophy Game in Tom Stoppard's *Professional Foul*', *Midwest Quarterly*, XXII (1981), p. 407-15.

Evelyn Cobley, 'Catastrophe Theory in Tom Stoppard's *Professional Foul*', *Contemporary Literature*, XXV (Spring 1984), p. 53-65.

Night and Day

Play in two acts.

First London production: Phoenix Th., 8 Nov. 1978 (dir. Peter Wood; with Diana Rigg, and subsequently Maggie Smith and Susan Hampshire as Ruth Carson).

First New York production: ANTA Th., 27 Nov. 1979 (dir. Peter Wood; with Maggie Smith).

Published: London: Faber, 1978; revised ed., 1979.

The action takes place in Kambawe, a former British Colony in Black Africa . . . in and around the house of Carson, a British colonial survivor who still runs the family's mines. He also has a challengingly attractive wife, Ruth, and a Telex machine and it would be hard to say which has the greater appeal for the three journalists who cluster around his jam-pot. They consist of a photographer-reporter team from the same paper, and an ambitious freelance, Milne, who has scooped an interview with the country's rebel leader shortly after quitting a newspaper in Grimsby. The plot is partly one of straight professional rivalry, with Wagner (the old pro) cunningly allowing Milne a second trip to the rebels while he sits tight to get a clandestine interview with the presidential dictator. But this is combined with two other simultaneous dramas. Wagner had a one-night affair in London with Carson's wife who is now drifting in the direction of the younger man. Also, Milne is known to Wagner (a staunch union man) as the 'Grimsby Scab', for his defiance of a journalists' strike and, in a beautifully-prepared final irony, the blacking of Milne's copy prevents the union militant from printing the greatest story of his life. At which point, the African war and the

wars of Fleet Street converge.
                              Irving Wardle, *'Night and Day', The Times*,
                                                  9 November 1978, p. 11

[*Night and Day* is] a naturalistic play. I had a perfectly sound
explanation for that as well, and a very mundane one. It was a
play which I wrote for Michael Codron because I'd promised him
a play ten years previously, and there were a number of consider-
ations which were more or less self-conscious ones, to do with one
set, and not too many actors, so that Michael Codron would be
able to do it as a West End manager. I mean, giving him a play
which started with fourteen acrobats wouldn't have pleased him.
And because it was a play about journalism, one of the few times
I've ever drawn on my own experience, even secondhand experience, because I didn't work on Fleet Street, I wanted to do a
naturalistic play. I was also interested by the way journalists tend
to ape their fictitious models. It's a certain way of behaving
which derives from 'tough' films. Of course, in naturalism there is
a reciprocal thing between the model and life, and in thinking
yes, yes, a play about journalists of some sort, again without a
great deal of thought, I fell into a way of thinking about the
material which led to a naturalistic play. . . .

The difference between *Night and Day* and *Travesties* is more
to do with structure than how I write. I find that people who saw
these two plays are divided [between] those who congratulate me
on getting past the 'hummingbird' phase and those who say 'What
are you *doing*? It's all naturalistic, with a beginning, a middle, and
an end!' . . .

My feelings about Wagner in particular and about journalism
are rather ambivalent, but I admire Wagner rather a lot as a character. I would admire him if he existed. I admire good profes-
sionals. I'm a bit of a journalistic groupie anyway. I think journalism is what Milne says it is, the last line of defence in this
country. And surrounding this approbation is the knowledge that
a great deal of journalism is despised and rightly so. I mean there
is a lot of abuse in the mouths of other characters, particularly
the woman. And she speaks for me as well. Nobody can have a
cut and dried good/bad attitude toward Wagner or journalism
because there are things to be said on different sides. She's a prej-
udiced observer with her own experience. . . .

In fact I would have thought that — if there is such a person —
the average watcher of this play would find that Milne carries
more conviction than Ruth. Ruth has got a gift for sarcastic

abuse, but what Milne says is true. I mean it is true: with a free press everything is correctible, however imperfect things are, they are correctible if people know they're going on. If we don't know they're going on, it's concealable: true. I believe it to be a true statement. Milne has my prejudice if you like. Somehow unconsciously, I wanted him to be known to be speaking the truth. . . . The press is a *real thing*, you know, papers are *real things* which you can *read*. And you like some of it and think it's important, and some of it you think is despicable. What one is trying to say is that a lot of it is hardly defensible but it's the price you pay for the part that matters.

Stoppard, 'Trad Tom Pops In', *Gambit*,
No. 37 (1981), p. 6, 11, 15

The best thing that can happen to a playwright is to discover that two plays he's been thinking about can actually be the same play. That way, with some luck, you can wind up with more than the sum of the two parts. Journalism was an interest of mine, I wanted to write a . . . love story, really, and finally the arcs intersected. . . . Unusually for me, there are things said in this play which utterly speak for me, things very much on the side of free journalism.

Robert Berkvist, 'This Time, Stoppard Plays It
(Almost) Straight', *New York Times*, 25 Nov. 1979,
Sec. II, p. 5

Would you tell me a little bit about the fantasy scene at the beginning of Act II?

My idea was to stage it as though it was absolutely real, not in half light or anything. And then for the revelation to be retro-active. I can't remember at what stage the thing changed its character. But I think that I rely too heavily on retroactive exposition and tend to alienate and baffle audiences if I follow through with it.

Yet it does seem to me that Ruth's fantasy heightens our sense of the way reality works more than the superficially accepted reality.

I like doing that a lot. The rationale is always rational, if you see what I mean. I don't think that it can be done for the sake of its own effect; ultimately it has to justify itself in rational terms for me. I must say that it hasn't always succeeded in the case of the audience for *Night and Day*. It seems to be difficult to do it right for everybody. Because of that we've been tinkering with the scene ever since the play opened – and not just that one, either. Because you know one found that people, some people weren't quite sure in some curious way – they weren't quite sure afterwards whether it was a fantasy or not. Although there was no way it couldn't be one.

> Stoppard, interviewed by Nancy Shields Hardin,
> *Contemporary Literature*, XXII (Spring 1981), p. 159-60

[Ruth's] persistent and lonely fantasies, part-pulp, part-desperation, show a benign yet cutting understanding of female sexuality, and one whose accuracy left my companion at the Phoenix last week ruefully astonished.

> Benedict Nightingale, 'Debriefing', *New Statesman*,
> 17 Nov. 1978, p. 672

This play is actually about *more* than press freedom – it is about freedom in general. . . . The final emotional and ethical weight of the piece is carried by Diana Rigg's brilliantly characterized Ruth Carson: this really is a portrayal in a thousand, a mixture of isolation, grandeur, vulnerability, and candour, laced with the wit with which all Stoppard characters seem almost cursed. It is Mrs. Carson who speaks most eloquently about freedom and yet it is she who is the least free of all the characters (even the glorified house-boy, Francis), enchained by marriage to a man whom she actually adores but does not love: by a self-style which denies her capabilities (capabilities which she makes admirably obvious); by life in a foreign country as the chattel and ornament of an anachronistic lifestyle; by an inability to indulge her sexual appetites without battering herself with rationalizations and doubts. . . . Tom Stoppard the feminist? Maybe not, but this is by far the strongest and most potent part that he has yet written for a woman.

> Steve Grant, *'Night and Day'*, *Plays and Players*,
> Jan. 1979, p. 18-19

The debate on press freedom

[Stoppard] loads the dice by making Wagner thick and crude and Milne a sexy heart-flutterer who also gets the story. And even when it comes to fundamental principles he uses steamrollering arguments. It's all very well for the engineer's wife to say that England is littered with papers pushing every political line from Mao to Mosley and that, if the big battalions dominate, that is simply the law of supply and demand. But he never grapples with the question as to whether profitability should determine the right to publish opinion or the common-sense fact that the bulk of the English national press supports one particular party. But it's a sign of the play's worth that one wants to argue with it. And on many journalistic issues Stoppard is both brilliant ad precise. He devastatingly parodies the way particular papers might report a foreign story. He conveys exactly the Lego-set language of some of the populars (Tug-of-Love Baby Mum in Pools Win). And he punctures journalistic ego by suggesting that a lot of Fleet Street writing is dictated by personal myth-making and that if printers often earn more than scribes there may be good reason for it.

Michael Billington, 'Night and Day', The Guardian,
9 Nov. 1978

What is equally impressive is the way Stoppard has re-written one or two scenes to make the discussion about press freedom much more even handed. My own initial objection to the play was that Stoppard's libertarian passion led to a debate about the press that was, in every sense, rigged. Ruth Carson, the mining engineer's wife in the fictitious African state of Kambawe, was allowed to run spectacular rings around Wagner, the hard-nosed Fleet Street advocate of the closed shop. Now Stoppard has re-written the second act debate so that it becomes a reported conversation between Ruth and her eight-year-old prep school son. This both gives the argument a comic perspective (Ruth makes wounding points while spreading her son's Marmite) and also suggests there are two sides to the issue, that Britain has papers pushing every possible line from Hitler to St. Francis of Assisi but that real power is still in the hands of vested economic interests.

Michael Billington, 'Night and Day', The Guardian,
5 July 1979, p. 8

See also: Judy Simons, *'Night and Day'*, *Gambit*, No. 37 (1981) p. 77-86.

Dogg's Hamlet, Cahoot's Macbeth

Two loosely-linked one-act plays

First production: Arts Centre, University of Warwick,
21 May 1979.

First London production: Collegiate Th., Bloomsbury, 17 July
1979.

First American production: Terrace Th., Kennedy Centre,
Washington, Sept. 1979.

First New York production: 22 Steps Th., 3 Oct. 1979.
(All productions by the British American Repertory Co.,
dir. Ed Berman.)

Published: London: Inter-Action Imprint, 1979; London:
Faber, 1980.

In Dogg's Hamlet *familiar words used in an unexpected context
take on a wholly new meaning: Wittgenstein, in fact, mates with
Brian Rix as a group of schoolboys and a theatrical removal
man erect a platform for a prize-giving. People addressed as
'cretinous git' smile warmly with approval, someone greeted
with 'Afternoon, squire' intemperately bristles and the guest of
honour graciously begins her speech with 'Scabs, slobs, black
yobs, yids, spicks, wops'. Words, in short, charge their sounds
while the logic of relationships and actions remains intact. It's a
good joke but for me nothing like as funny as what it leads to,
which is a fifteen-minute version of* Hamlet *that completely
retains the plot and structure of the play. Hamlet just has time
for the first line of 'To be or not to be'. Ophelia rushes in crying
'My lord' and is peremptorily told 'Get thee to a nunnery'. The
effect is of a speeded-up Keystone Cops technique applied to the
Bard or of seeing the whole plot of* Hamlet *pass before your eyes
while you are drowning. Spurred to an encore, the cast then do a
ninety-second repeat of the whole play. It is a beautiful scholarly
jape.*

*[*Cahoot's Macbeth*] is derived from an actual situation in
Czechoslovakia: proscribed actors turn up in one's sitting-room
and perform for oneself and friends a truncated* Macbeth. *Stoppard
poses just such a situation with interruptions from a clodhopping
cop who has picked up the theatrical jargon ('Is this phone
practical?') and from the theatrical removal man who pops up*

unexpectedly as Banquo's Ghost or the Third Murderer. The problem is the situation Stoppard describes is already bizarre: to decorate it even further is not only to paint the lily but to pull it apart as well. . . . An ingenious attempt to combine Shakespeare, linguistic jokes, political comment and zany farce.
Michael Billington, *'Dogg's Hamlet, Cahoot's Macbeth'*,
The Guardian, 17 July 1979, p. 8

[Stoppard's 'Preface' explains that *'Dogg's Hamlet* derives from a section of Wittgenstein's philosophical investigations. . . . The appeal to me consisted in the possibility of writing a play which had to teach the audience the language the play was written in'. *Cahoot's Macbeth* is based on the situation of the Czech playwright, Pavel Kohout, and some actors in his country. Unable to work, a group of five began performing an abridged *Macbeth* in people's homes.]

There are two basic jokes in Tom Stoppard's *Dogg's Hamlet*, one for each part of the play. The first is that language is an arbitrary form of signification and therefore susceptible to humorous mutation if words are ascribed different meanings from those they normally possess. The second, which also depends upon incongruity for its effect, is that the action and famous lines of a well-known play can be made to appear quite ridiculous if stripped of all incidental substance and performed at breakneck speed. . . .Were [*Cahoot's Macbeth*] written by anyone with less immaculate credentials, the play might seem offensive and the motives behind it dubious. As it is, one can only conclude that the combination of seriousness and absurdity is miscalculated and the result different from what was intended.
Colin Ludlow, *'Dogg's Hamlet, Cahoot's Macbeth'*,
Plays and Players, Aug. 1979, p. 28

The evening as a whole leaves a sketchier, more fragmented, and finally less eloquent impression than what I take to be Stoppard's most successful foray into committed hilarity, the TV play *Professional Foul*. Both are about usurpation and the abuse of power, not unlike *Macbeth* itself; but it is the one that ignores, not the one that explicitly invokes, that parallel which comes the nearer to justifying it.

Benedict Nightingale, 'Git Away', *New Statesman*,
20 July 1979, p. 105

Also see:

C.J. Gianakaris, 'Stoppard's Adaptations of Shakespeare: *Dogg's Hamlet, Cahoot's Macbeth'*, *Comparative Drama*, XVII (Fall 1984), p. 22-40.

Phyllis Ruskin and John H. Lutterbie, 'Balancing the Equation', *Modern Drama*, XXVI (Dec. 1983), p. 543-54 [Stoppard in San Diego for rehearsals of *Dogg's Hamlet, Cahoot's Macbeth*].

The Real Thing

Play in two acts.

First production: Strand Th., London, 16 Nov. 1982 (dir. Peter Wood; with Roger Rees as Henry and Felicity Kendal as Annie).

First New York production: Plymouth Th,, 5 Jan. 1984 (dir. Mike Nichols; with Jeremy Irons as Henry and Glenn Close as Annie).

Published: London: Faber, 1982.

Henry, successful author of a play called House of Cards *(an image culled from reviews of Stoppard's plays), falls for Annie, an actress whose husband is playing in Henry's comedy. And in the opening scenes you can already observe Stoppard clearing an area of surprise and lucidity in a jungle of romantic cliché. The actual infidelity follows a fictional infidelity; when it comes to making the break, Annie simply announces: 'It's only a couple of marriages and a child.' Nor is there any obligatory scene with the deserted wife and child: the next we see of them is two years later, when they are all on the most friendly terms.*

In taking on Annie, however, Henry is also lumbering himself with a cause: that of a young soldier, Brodie, who has been jailed for desecrating the Cenotaph. The cause languishes, but Brodie writes a play about it which, to Henry's immense discomfort, Annie requires him to knock into performable shape. This scene between them consists of a classic statement of the eternal art-versus-truth debate. For Annie, the fact that Brodie has written of his gut experiences is all that counts. For Henry, all that counts is that he is a dreadful writer. He picks up a cricket bat, an artefact, he says, as carefully sprung as a ballroom floor. 'We', he says, 'are trying to write cricket bats, so that when we throw up an idea and give it a little knock it might travel.' There speaks the old Stoppard, and it is sad to see his spokesman climbing down, doing the rewrite, and suffering ecstasies of jealous desolation when Annie embarks on an affair with the actor who is playing Brodie's alter ego.

Brodie himself, who finally arrives in loutish person for his television debut, is singularly ungrateful. And, before he winds up unmasked and with a bowl of dip over his face, he has time to dismiss Henry's improvements as mere cleverness. . . . We get further fictional inserts; a subtext of the parts Annie is getting, complete with rehearsed readings of Miss Julie *(downward mobility, matching the Brodie relationship) and* 'Tis Pity She's a Whore *(matching the incestuous fiction/reality betrayals). . . . Polly Adams, very sharp and growly as the abandoned wife [Charlotte], and Jeremy Clyde, succumbing to torrential self-pity as the abandoned husband [Max], are much missed when they fade away.*

Irving Wardle 'Cleverness with its Back to the Wall',
The Times, 17 Nov. 1982

In The Real Thing, *the playwright makes a statement about not being able to write about love. Is that you talking about yourself?*

I was talking about myself before writing *The Real Thing*. The play contains self-reference jokes. Henry says when he tries to write a play about love, it comes out 'embarrassing, childish, or rude'. The love story, as I wrote it, tries to avoid banality while suggesting it. Henry says in the same scene, 'It makes me nervous to see three-quarters of a page and no writing on it. I talk better than this.' That's self-reference.

That's the closest you've come to writing about love?

Yes. *Night and Day* was a first go at it. As far as I'm concerned, this is all I'll do. For better or worse, that's it — the love play! I've been aware of the process that's lasted 25 years, of shedding inhibitions about self-revelation. I wouldn't have dreamed of writing it about ten years ago, but as you get older, you think, who cares?'

> Stoppard, interviewed by Mel Gussow, *New York Times Magazine*, 1 Jan. 1984, Sec. VI, p. 18-23, 28

Actors on their roles
[Roger Rees conceived Henry] as being very Russian — 'great swoops of emotion, from the very high to the very low.' . . . He starts out over-confident because he's having an affair and he's happily looked after by a sort of mother-figure, his present wife. But in the end he has to learn to deal with the true nature of a relationship. Luckily enough he is just saved.

> Roger Rees, quoted by Patrick Ensor,
> 'An Actor at the Sheepdog Trials', *The Guardian*,
> 12 Nov. 1982, p. 9

[Jeremy Irons found Henry] a wonderful role, because it allows me to play a great range, from flippant comedy to deeply felt pain. Personally, it touched me; it said things about love and commitment that I felt but couldn't possibly say because I don't have the brilliance Tom Stoppard has. . . . I sort of instinctively knew Henry. I like his lack of self-consciousness, and the way he has a craft that he's good at. I like his boyishness; there's a lot of the child in Henry, and I've always believed that in every man there's a little boy trying to get out. . . . During the course of the play, Henry realizes that Annie's ideas are valid just because they're hers, and that the fact that he can argue them out and win the argument doesn't mean they're any less valid.

> Jeremy Irons, quoted by Leslie Bennetts,
> 'Irons Identifies with *Real Thing* Role', *New York Times*,
> 9 Jan. 1984, Sec. C, p. 13

[Kenneth Welsh, playing Max in New York found the role] a feed for the essential thing the play is about, which is Henry's adventures in loveland. Tom Stoppard has a tendency to focus on one thing, and make the other roles subservient to it. This was so much the case in *Night and Day* that I turned down the role of the photographer, which was offered to me. But here, with Max, there's a schizophrenic quality to the man. In the first scene he's playing a character in one of Henry's plays, and I have to imagine myself being Max imagining how to play that role. He has a life of his own.

> Kenneth Welsh, quoted by Ray Conlogue,
> 'Welsh on Broadway', *Toronto Globe and Mail*,
> 4 Feb. 1984, Sec. E, p. 3

The critics on the characters
There is a stunning performance by Roger Rees as Henry: all nervous impulse and growing panic as he grabs at a telephone, claws at a book-case, or simply follows Annie's departure from a room with hopeless resignation. Felicity Kendal's Annie also subtly combines impishness and passion, surrender to the moment and rock-fast affection.

> Michael Billington, *'The Real Thing'*, The Guardian,
> 17 Nov. 1982

Stoppard is still, it seems, unable to create a leading woman character who is a fully convincing human being, although he has shown on several occasions that he can give good actresses interesting things to do and amusing lines to speak.

> Richard Findlater, *'The Real Thing'*, Plays and Players,
> Jan. 1983, p. 27

In Peter Wood's original London production, play was the thing. Though no character's emotion was stinted, that *Real Thing* emphasized the artifice. It might have been written not by Stoppard but by Henry himself. It might even have taken place inside the Alpine glass globe the architect shakes at the end of the *House of Cards* scene. As Stoppard notes, 'The set [by Carl Toms] was more stylized, with a series of screens used to reveal each scene. Peter saw a spare set with a Japanese feeling.' (For the Broadway version, Tony Walton has designed a revolving stage of handsome, naturalistic sets that look very much lived in). . . . Rees's Henry was an audacious interpretation: the artist as manic-depressive child. Henry is, after all, a little boy in love with the sound of his own mind. . . . Still, there is something adolescent about the intensity of Henry's ardor, whether for the sweetest pop music from the mid-1960s (his own teenage years) or for his one-gal-guy idealism (the play describes Annie as 'very much like the woman whom Charlotte has ceased to be', so in effect Henry has been faithful to his *belle ideale* by switching mates). As this little boy lost in the web of words and wonders, Rees was a jumping-jack joy. Jeremy Irons's Henry could be Rees's father. The achievement of Irons and director Mike Nichols is to secure Henry's foibles in the heart of a mature male. He's a believer who's never lost that lovin' feeling. There is a fierce longing in the gaze Irons directs either at Annie or at a blank piece of paper in his typewriter. Where Rees leapt from rapture to desperation, Irons takes small, careful steps. 'Roger is a more energetic, neurotic kind of actor', Irons says. 'I generally don't like giving more than is required. If a moment requires A, I won't give A plus 3 just so my technique can dazzle the audience.'

Richard Corliss, 'Stoppard in the Name of Love',
Time, 16 Jan. 1984, p. 67

Those who have viewed both productions generally contend that Jeremy Irons as Stoppard's protagonist in New York is better than Roger Rees in London because Irons is more vulnerable and because there is more sexual chemistry in his relationship with Annie. . . . To me, Roger Rees was more convincing as an intellectual who could reel off Mr. Stoppard's lines and Henry's plays. Because he had that stature, his personal pain was more harrowing (watered-down Aristotle on the tragic hero here) and his ascent to self-knowledge more moving.

Holly Hill, 'Stoppard Still Accelerating',
The Times, 16 Feb. 1984, p. 9

Style and themes
On the surface, it appears initially as a retreat into Noel Cowardy naturalism: surprising in a writer who has vigorously attacked the 'fallacy' of naturalism and its consequences in 'bad theatre, bad thinking, and bad feeling'. But the orthodoxy of form and content is (like so much in Mr. Stoppard's work) deceptive; and he again uses the distorting mirror of theatrical pastiche, and the echoes of plays within a play, to mix reflections of actuality and illusion, juggle with ideas and explore the relationship of art to other kinds of reality.

Richard Findlater, as above, p. 26

It's a romantic comedy of a tragic nature, corresponding perhaps most closely to less successful attempts in this same field recently made by our other two leading British dramatists, Harold Pinter (in *Betrayal*) and Peter Nichols (in *Passion Play*). Likc them, it's a story of rearranged marriages and furniture in the affluent London architect-and-actor belt; in its first Cowardly moments we get what appears to be a stylish comedy of bad manners, full of cuckoo-clock jokes about Old Basle and Swiss Frank, but no sooner are we getting used to those *Private Lives* than we realize that they're not what the play is about at all. . . . *The Real Thing* is also love, and divorce, and jealousy, and innocence, and anguish, and in writing about all of that within the context of a marital drama about an actress and a playwright Mr. Stoppard has come up with the warmest and the most touching play he has ever written. In a purely artistic sense, this is also an autobiographical play since it is about a dramatist trying to write a play about indescribable love.

Sheridan Morley, *Shooting Stars*
(London, 1983), p. 338-9

[Brodie] made his protest to ingratiate himself with Annie; Annie supports him because she feels guilty; Henry helps them because he loves Annie. These, anyway, are the play's final revelations, and their inference leaves me boggling. Am I deranged when I wonder if it's morally acceptable to aim H-bombs at Moscow? Is Tom merely sublimating childhood feelings of rejection when he writes indignant plays about the abuse of human rights in his native Czechoslovakia and elsewhere? Must we dismiss the campaigns of, say, Wilberforce, Silverman and Sakharov as emotionally dishonest 'postures'?

Benedict Nightingale, 'On the Couch',
New Statesman, 26 Nov. 1982, p. 30

Stoppard turns some of his best verbal fire against the kind of cant and half-truth to which the Left is prone. The mistake he makes, or the play makes, it seems to me, is confusing the cant and the cause. His playwright hero defends brilliantly and wittily his conviction that to be a writer you need, not a cause, but the skills of a writer. His adversary is permitted to put, but with no comparable eloquence, the counter-statement that to have the skills of a writer and nothing to say is not exactly a position of strength. What comfort will there be for those who attack (as Stoppard's play does) the failings of the language in which the anti-nuclear argument is put, if that argument proves nevertheless to be correct?

C.K. Stead, 'Diary', *London Review of Books*,
18-31 Oct. 1984, p. 25

Towards the end it begins to look as though it is the soldier's
slovenly deportment, his greedy fingers squelching in the salmon
dip, his contemptuous fist grabbing the hooch, which is held
against him. But surely the man who in another major work of
modern literature penetrated the minds of Lenin, Joyce and
Tristran Tzara, wouldn't stoop to vilifying a character with
mere snobbery. Would he? The fact is that Stoppard is the Great
Comforter of the middle class. If you were upset by the circum-
stances of Barry Prosser's death, or queried the new powers of
the police to distrain your liberty, here is a man with the impec-
cable credentials of spending the first two years of his life in
Czechoslovakia to tell you how much more horrible the KGB
would be. And he will do more. He can go on to consecrate every
petty and craven feature of his adopted class as not merely the
best of humanity but the very definition of it. All else is reduced
to barbarism.

Michael Stewart, 'Great Comforter',
Tribune, 3 Dec. 1982, p. 9

Also see:
Hersch Zeifman, 'Comedy of Ambush: Tom Stoppard's *The Real
Thing*', *Modern Drama*, XXVI (June 1983), p. 139-49.

The Dog It Was that Died

Play for radio (65 minutes).
Transmitted: BBC Radio 3, 9 Dec. 1982 (dir. John Tydeman).
Published: in *The Dog It Was that Died and Other Plays*
   (London: Faber, 1983).
Tape: BBC 'Plays on Tape', 1984.

The Dog It Was that Died *delves into what one of its protagonists
calls 'the English character' – the upper-crust manners and
mentality of the nation that has so warmed to Stoppard's talent.
It is a comic spy story, setting up in the opening minutes a*

handful of conundrums which are unravelled – with varying degrees of predictability – in the subsequent hour. Rupert Purvis is a British intelligence officer undergoing 'a bit of a crise'. Having become a double agent, he had doubled and redoubled so often that he has lost track of whether or not he is a traitor. Just before attempting suicide, he posts a letter revealing apparently scandalous facts about close colleagues. The inevitable investigation causes none of the ructions Purvis expects. . . . As the truth about his position emerges, the play neatly satirizes bluff and counter-bluff in espionage as it echoes the bellicose stalemate of international relations. . . . There are skirmishes to savour when Purvis tests his delinquent ideas against what passes for the philosophy of his British superior. . . . On each of its levels, the play asks what was done as well as whodunnit. As Purvis does not know what effect his professional activities are having, what moral judgment can be made of him? Might the British look less kindly on his befuddlement if he were causing more damage and proving less susceptible to their manipulations?

Jim Hiley, 'Double Trouble', *The Listener*,
2 Dec. 1982, p. 28

Together with Beckett and Pinter, Stoppard is one of the writers who use [radio] most imaginatively. . . . He enjoys doing what can't be done on any other medium. . . . There's a scene in which a crane is lowering an obelisk on to the octagonal Gothic tower of a folly, and another scene in a drawing-room, where a woman who runs a donkey-sanctuary is trying to put stitches into a prostrate and neighing donkey which has just undergone surgery. Theoretically, cinema could accommodate these sequences, but they would not be so comic if we could see the dog and the donkey. We also get a beautifully funny climax, characteristic of radio comedy at its best, when the woman's husband lets go of the donkey's legs to pick up a pair of forceps from the grate, drops them because they're too hot, gets kicked, and as he yells in agony, his collection of clocks starts chiming. Radio also brings Stoppard's love of wordplay to the fore.

Ronald Hayman, 'Double Entendres of a Double-Agent',
Times Literary Supplement, 24 Dec. 1982, p. 1419

Squaring the Circle

Documentary-drama for television (115-minutes).
Transmitted: Channel 4, 31 May 1984.
Published: with *Every Good Boy Deserves Favour* and
  Professional Foul (London: Faber, 1984).

Charts the events in Poland between August 1980, when Solid-
arity launched its campaign for trade union rights within the
Communist state, and December 1981, when martial law was
declared. Stoppard employs some risky dramatic tricks in order
to explain political developments – and they work: the division
of Poland by outside powers is illustrated by two men pushing
bread rolls around a cafe table: talks between Walesa, Glemp,
and Jaruzelski are conducted over a game of cards; and at one
point a group of Russian politicians are transformed suddenly
into a Mafia gang. The action takes place mainly on a set with a
red carpet and steel scaffolding (by the Polish-born designer
Voytek) which becomes the Gdansk shipyard, the Vatican, or
Brezhnev's office.

Susie Cornfield, 'TV Previews', *Sunday Times*,
27 May 1984, p. 52

[At the beginning of 1982] a producer named Fred Brogger suggested that I should write a television film about Solidarity.
Thus began a saga, only moderately exceptional by these standards, which has gone through four or five scripts, and eight
directors (one of them twice), and has resulted in two versions
. . . one for Britain and one for America. . . . Documentary fiction
is always in danger of seeming to claim to know more than a film
maker *can* know. . . . That led me to the idea of having a narrator
with *acknowledged fallibility*. . . . At various times, *Squaring the*
Circle was going to be filmed on location in Hamburg, Liverpool,
Helsinki, or, alternatively, when we seemed to have missed the
snow in Hamburg, Liverpool, and even Helsinki, on numberless
reconstructions in different studios. It was going to have lots of
ambience, or it was going to be enclosed in a series of rooms; it
was going to be as immaculate as a Hollywood movie or as
exciting as newsreel shot from the hip; it was going to star international names or it was going to be made with totally unknown

75

actors. . . . [Voytek's set] perfectly expressed the qualified reality which I had been worrying about creating since starting to write. . . . In the end, *Squaring the Circle* cost £1,264,661. By that time everything was in dollars.

Stoppard, 'Lech's Troubles with Chuck, Bruce, and Bob',
The Times, 31 May 1984, p. 14

A nervous disciplined attempt to suppress everything that makes a (Stoppard) play worth watching, in favour of a political diagram, for export only. Stoppard's hero-worship of Walesa turned him into a cut-out.

Hugo Williams, 'New Moon', *New Statesman*,
8 June 1984, p. 32

It was as if Stoppard was trying to represent, in theatrical terms, the strangely inconsistent traits — fierce conservatism, activism, fatalism, passion, and cynicism — which foreigners sometimes claim to observe in the Polish character.

John Naughton, 'Coming Unstuck',
The Listener, 7 June 1984, p. 27

b: Adaptations

Tango

Play by Slawomir Mrozek (1965), translated with
Nicholas Bethell.
First production: Royal Shakespeare Co. at Aldwych
Th., London, 25 May 1966 (dir. Trevor Nunn).
Published: London: Cape, 1968; and in *Three East
European Plays*, ed. Martin Esslin (Harmondsworth:
Penguin, 1970).

It was only about a fortnight before rehearsals were due to begin that the director, Trevor Nunn, called in extra help (me) to make the dialogue more speakable. Bethell's advantage was that he could read Polish and mine was supposed to be that I could write dialogue. [My translation was] made as faithful as possible . . . too faithful in fact. The play obviously didn't work as

well in English as it had worked in the original.
Stoppard, letter quoted in Richard Corballis,
Stoppard: the Mystery and the Clockwork (Oxford:
Amber Lane, 1984), p. 169-70

The House of Bernarda Alba

Play by Garcia Lorca (*c*. 1936).
First production: Greenwich Th., London, 22 Mar. 1973
(dir. Robin Phillips).
Unpublished (Richard Carballis has been unable to find a
surviving copy, p. 174).

I don't know any Spanish at all. Lorca has already decided what
the play is about and how it works. I think of myself as an
adaptor. It's a very faithful adaptation. I've worked from two
principal sources. One is the Penguin, done in the 'forties, which
has the great virtue of telling you what Lorca wrote, word for
word, whether it's actually *speakable* or not. For example,
Bernarda comes in while a great uproar is going on. The original
is something like 'What a poverty I have, not having a flash of
lightning between my fingers'. I've made this: 'My God I am poor
in means to pay you — I should have the power to strike you
dead with my raised finger'. That's an extreme example, but there
are dozens of minor examples, smaller difficulties. One of the
problems is that the translations seem to be more genteel than
I'm told the Spanish is. There's so much sexual frustration in the
play one has tended to get more frustrations than sexuality. . . .
This is where my second source comes in — I have a literal translation from a girl who has been reading Spanish and drama at
Bristol University. Her name's Katie Kendall and she's also
supplied me with notes and some of her ideas as well. . . . The
play is full of horrific images, and by a careful choice of words
one puts into it what is *understood* in the original. As an adaptor
I try to make a line work as it should work. I'm trying to think
of an image that explains this. Think of your own mind as a
tuning-fork. A piano sounds wrong. You go through it string by
string to make the instrument sound right in your mind. But one
has a brain, not a tuning-fork. The sound, unfortunately, begins
to influence the tuning-fork. . . .

The whole knack of adaptation — you're faced with many
alternatives but only one choice is right. *That's* the abstract idea

of translation, I suppose. The problem one faces with translations is the more free you get the more natural it sounds. The more literal the less natural. These two lines have to come to some sort of a deal. You have to find out where to cross the freedom line, where the fidelity line. Another danger is that you actually can iron out inflection and phrases which make the situation Spanish. You fall into a trap and it all slides off into a kind of 'Knightsbridge'. . . . To adapt Lorca you need to be a poet, a playwright and fluent in Spanish — and I'm only one of those things!

> Stoppard, quoted by Michael Leech, 'The Translators',
> *Plays and Players*, April 1973, p. 37-8

Three Men in a Boat

Adaptation of Jerome K. Jerome's comic novel (1889) as a television film.
Transmitted: BBC-2, 31 Dec. 1975 (dir. Stephen Frears: with Tim Curry as J., Stephen Moore as George, and Michael Palin as Harris).

I didn't grow up loving the book, as so many people seem to have done, so I hadn't preconceptions about what were its officially funniest moments.

> Stoppard, quoted by David Pryce-Jones, 'To Say Nothing
> of the Dog', *Radio Times*, 18 Dec. 1975, p. 109

In the main Stoppard responded soberly to Jerome, removing a great deal and too often replacing big bad jokes with more sophisticated, but smaller, jokes of his own. Stephen Frear is an excellent director (*Gumshoe, A Day Out*) but he did not find a comic style faithful to both writers.

> Michael Ratcliffe, 'Playing a Very Straight Bat',
> *The Times*, 2 Jan. 1976, p. 5

Undiscovered Country

'Version' in five acts of *Das Weite Land*, by Arthur Schnitzler (1911), written with John Harrison.
First production: National Th., 20 June 1979 (dir. Peter Wood).

Published: London: Faber, 1980

The key line is a reference to 'A bogus civility between people made wretched by jealousy'; what the play shows us is couples indulging in a polite sexual excuse-me behind which lurks panic, death and an insane preoccupation with honour. The central figure, Friedrich Hofreiter, is a manufacturer of incandescent light bulbs who constantly seems to be switching other people off. One friend has already plunged to death while mountain climbing; as the play starts a Russian concert-pianist in love with Hofreiter's wife has strangely committed suicide; and the action works towards a duel between Friedrich and a young naval lieutenant who has casually cuckolded him. Baldly described, it sounds like a study of a Viennese Leontes. But what is fascinating is that the action is conducted against a background of tennis-parties, trips to the Dolomites, charade-like affaires, and summerhouse banter against Art Deco panels. Everything suggests a world of golden leisure and civilized deceit. But what Schnitzler shows us is the corrosive effect of habitual lying on this *Smiles of a Summer Night* atmosphere and the destructive impact of the hero's contaminated sense of honour.

> Michael Billington, 'Vintage Viener Schnitzler',
> *The Guardian*, 21 June 1979

Stoppard's translation of the title of Arthur Schnitzler's *Das Weite Land* as *Undiscovered Country* is worth a moment's thought. It is a neat English title, with various associations of which Hamlet's line about death being 'an undiscovered country' is the most immediate. In that 'To be or not to be' speech Hamlet also links death with sleep; and since Schnitzler was a contemporary of Freud, who had one or two things to say about sleeping and dreaming, the title aptly points to those 'intuitions' which Freud admired in Schnitzler. You can plough in other overtones and undertexts which Stoppard may or may not have intended — that, to the British, the Austro-Hungarian empire which Schnitzler so defiantly came to represent for theatregoers, was an undiscovered country, a source of wonder, mystery, and some rather snobbish amusement, with its old-fashioned duels, its quaint, over-formal manners and airs of ripe decadence. At the same time, you do not have to be an accomplished linguist to realize that Stoppard's title is not a literal translation of Schnitzler's, which means the 'wide' country. The question then arises as to

79

whether Stoppard's English version may not be an improvement on Schnitzler's German, because it does hold these connotations of death, sleep, and the soul, the strange inner landscape with which Schnitzler's play is concerned.

John Elsom, 'Missing Links',
The Listener, 5 July 1979, p. 24

What he conveys here, as he did in *Rosencrantz and Guildenstern Are Dead*, is his own understanding that the most interesting issue is not the enigmatic unpredictability of people's souls but the profound attraction of death.

J.P. Stern, 'Anyone for Tennis, Anyone for Death?',
Encounter, LIII (Oct. 1979), p. 27-9

On the Razzle

Play in three acts adapted from *Einen Jux will er sich machen*, by Johann Nestroy (1842), using a literal translation by Neville and Stephen Plaice.
First London production: National Th. at the Lyttelton, 22 Sept. 1981 (dir. Peter Wood).
First American production: Arena Stage, Washington, Nov. 1982.
Published: London: Faber, 1981.

[Two grocer's assistants seek pleasure on an unofficial day off in Vienna; their employer, with a new uniform and a new servant, is also in the city. Scottish Fortnight is in progress; other characters include thwarted lovers and a sex-starved coachman.] All the main characters and most of the plot come from Nestroy but almost none of the dialogue attempts to offer a translation of what Nestroy wrote. . . . *On the Razzle* makes no use of dialect, ignores period flavour in dialogue, and has no songs. It is still set in Vienna (though about fifty years later than *Einen Jux*) but not essentially so. The two essentials which this play takes from the original are, firstly, the almost mythic tale of two country mice escaping to town for a day of illicit freedom, adventure, mishap, and narrow escapes from discovery; and, secondly, the prime concern to make this tale as comic an entertainment as possible.

Stoppard, 'Introduction', p. 7

The Nestroy was a holiday after the Schnitzler but it was more difficult and took much longer. . . . Although the Nestroy play also includes many denser and sustained speeches enjoying great liberality of language, for similar reasons the translator has to give himself an equal liberality; which is why it was a holiday as well as hard work. . . . I was stuck much of the time as I am with a play of my own because there was so much more necessary invention, and declared invention at that; my inventions for *Undiscovered Country* were guilty secrets, almost admissions of failure, bits of non-Schnitzler trying not to look un-Schnitzler, put in because I couldn't make the thing bounce properly. But with *On the Razzle* I abandoned quite early on the onus of conveying Nestroy intact into English. I'm not really a believer in the hypothesis of true translation. The particularity of a writer's voice is a mysterious collusion of sound and sense. The certain knowledge that a translation will miss it by at least an inch makes it less dreadful to miss it by a yard.

Stoppard, 'Across Nestroy with Map and Compass,'
programme note to National Theatre production

Everything and everyone is there for farcical purposes only, and purposes which are vitiated in three main ways. First, Stoppard and his director, Peter Wood, display a somewhat promiscuous appetite for comic incident and sub-plot. The principal strands and the main questions we should be asking — will master-grocer Zangler catch his truant employees, will he find the niece who has absconded with an unwished-for lover? — too often get submerged, forgotten. . . . Second, Dinsdale Landen replaces what's mean, tyrannical and potentially punitive in Zangler's character with a sort of goofy complacency, making it impossible to believe it would matter if he rumbled his disobedient underlings. Again, the tension of the main plot is dissipated; and, without tension, danger, the threat of disaster, farce simply can't function. Third, it's hard to respond to raw comic event when your ears are turning somersaults lest they miss some pun, some spoonerism, some erotic innuendo, or some other conceit or trick in what is, even by Stoppard's standards, a verbally hyperactive script. I myself found this doubly distracting, since I regard Stoppard's wit as a precious resource, but one, like gold or oil, that must also be finite. How could he squander so many clever, nonreusable lines on what is — let's say it — an enterprise at best

frivolous, at worst confused and silly?
>> Benedict Nightingale, 'Theatre', *New Statesman*,
>> 2 Oct. 1981, p. 27

Apart from *Jumpers* and *The Importance of being Earnest* there may be no script in English funnier than *On the Razzle*. From political farce and philosophical farce Mr. Stoppard has turned to writing farcical farce: both a raging example of the genre and a tribute to it. . . . What makes *On the Razzle* unique is that every line in it is either a joke or part of one.
>> Robert Cushman, 'Stoppard on the Razzle',
>> *The Observer*, 27 Sept. 1981

The Love for Three Oranges

Translation of libretto for Prokofiev's opera (1921).
First production: Glyndebourne Touring Opera, 8 Oct. 1983.

Prokofiev's *Oranges* could not be more deliciously served than in Tom Stoppard's pithy new translation which squeezes every ounce of flavour from Frank Corsaro's zestful staging. Mr. Stoppard has certainly garnered a rosette or two, for not only do his English words readily register with the audience, but his jokes (whether awful or elevated) whip up the froth in Gozzi's original and Prokofiev's treatment of it. . . . Stoppard's translation is appropriately unpretentious, though not above private games. Oddly, nobody laughed when the King's wizard, Chelio, says he's 'the real thing'. Other samples: 'I'm dreaming of an orange Christmas'; Truffaldino's 'It would be useless, not to say fruit-less'; Leander's 'She turned out to be a lemon, and has given him the pip — geddit?'
>> Tom Sutcliffe, *The Guardian*, 10 Oct. 1983, p. 11

Rough Crossing

Free adaptation of *Play at the Castle*, by Ferenc Molnar
   (1926), also known in English as *The Play's the Thing*
   (translated by P.G. Wodehouse).
First London production: National Th. at the Lyttelton,

30 Oct. 1984 (dir. Peter Wood).
Published: London: Faber, 1985.

What happens in the Molnar is that a young composer is heart-broken at hearing his fiancee is making love to another man: a manipulative playwright rescues the situation by turning life into art and dashing off a mock-Sardou playlet incorporating the overheard dialogue. But Stoppard translates the fragile action from a Mediterranean castle to transatlantic liner on board which a couple of Hungarian-born writers and a composer are trying to find the perfect ending for a Broadway musical comedy. Once again an emotional crisis is averted by the incorporation of a real-life love scene into the show; but the crucial difference is that most of Stoppard's second act is taken up with an extended parody of a 'twenties' musical that gradually sinks under the weight of its own Byzantine complexity. Stoppard seems, in a nutshell, to have missed the point of the Molnar. His play is about the power of illusion; and its most effective Pirandellian moment comes at the end of the second act when three alternative endings are tried before the curtain finally falls. Stoppard, however, sacrifices Molnar's playful artifice in order to do a jocular pastiche of an inextricable period musical about jewel thieves and white slave markets. . . . In Stoppard there are always the jokes. And initially these seem quite promising with the transformation of Molnar's Dvornichek from an omniscient footman into a land-based cabin steward who obstinately refers to the ship's verandah and first balcony.

> Michael Billington, *'Rough Crossing'*,
> *The Guardian*, 31 Oct. 1984

I've done three adaptations now. They are separate, but it's not really a separation between serious plays and adaptations; it's really a separation between my own original work whether serious or comic and work derived from other authors. There is even so a good deal of invention, as I've explained, not more than a dozen lines of *Rough Crossing* will compare with the original dialogue. I welcome adaptations for the good reason that I don't have continual ideas for new plays and it's nice to do a play in between where the idea is dropped in my lap.

> Stoppard, quoted by Robert Gore-Langton, 'Sea-Sickness
> at the National', *Plays and Players*, Oct. 1984, p. 17

a: Film Scripts

The Romantic Englishwoman
with Thomas Wiseman, from Wiseman's novel (dir. Joseph Losey; with Glenda Jackson, Michael Caine and Helmut Berger). *Released:* 1975.

Despair
from Vladimir Nabokov's novel (dir. Rainer Werner Fassbinder; with Dirk Bogarde). *Released:* 1978.

The Human Factor
from Graham Greene's novel (dir. Otto Preminger; with Richard Attenborough, Nicol Williamson, John Gielgud, Derek Jacobi, and Robert Morley). *Released:* 1980.

Brazil
with Terry Gilliam and Charles McKeown (dir. Terry Gilliam; with Jonathan Pryce, Ian Holm, Michael Palin, and Robert de Niro). *Released:* 1985.

b: Fiction

'Reunion', 'Life, Times: Fragments', 'The Story', in *Introduction 2: Stories by New Writers* (London: Faber, 1964), p. 121-36. [Three short stories.]

Lord Malquist and Mr. Moon
London: Anthony Blond, 1966; Panther, 1968; Faber, 1974. [Moon, who carries an inherited bomb and has an unconsumated marriage to Jane, works for Lord Malquist, to record his life and sayings. There are various other bizarre characters; it is the day of Churchill's funeral.]

Stoppard has written very little about his work. Though he has frequently given interviews, these have largely turned on the same few points: his difficulty in finding ideas; ideas, not plot or character, as his starting-point; his readiness to accept commissions; his ability to see both sides of issues. Strikingly, a new concern with social issues enters his plays in 1977. Full details of sources cited by short titles below may be found in Section a of 'Select Bibliography', below.

On language and the visual in theatre

[I have] an enormous love of language itself. For a lot of writers the language they use is merely a fairly efficient tool. For me the particular use of a particular word in the right place, or a group of words in the right order, to create a particular effect is important; it gives me more pleasure than to make a point which I might consider to be profound. On the other hand, when one does concentrate mainly on the language itself, with luck this appears to have some meaning, often in a general sense and, when one is very lucky, in a universal sense. . . . I have never achieved through words a moment in a theatre which would even approach the extraordinary feeling created by Peter Brook's *US* when a few white butterflies started to flap around the auditorium and one, the last one taken out of a tin, was set aflame. I shall never forget that; it's a useful corrective whenever I start feeling a certain indulgence towards the idea of language as an end in itself. And I do think in visual terms — not in terms of colours, or an actual stage, but certainly in terms of movement.

'Something to Declare',
Sunday Times, 25 Feb. 1968, p. 47

On choice of subject

As for real social stuff which makes headlines, I haven't got the slightest desire to write about it on its own terms. One thing that had an enormous effect on me was the evidence at the trial of the people who killed three Civil Rights workers at Meridian, Mississippi [in 1964]. I couldn't get out of my head the awful fact of those murders; but I couldn't begin to write about that kind of a subject in real terms. I think what I would write about if I ever got to the subject at all would be the fact that I was so personally revolted and disturbed by the cold-blooded killing of those three people that I'd like to get the people who did it and cold-bloodedly kill them.

'Something to Declare', as above

As a 'reactionary' writer

I think of myself as a reactionary in many ways. When I am struck by something I want to write about it; very often it doesn't appear to have much to do with my main existence. It doesn't reflect what I've been reading in the newspapers or any of my own preoccupations. I am preoccupied rather more with things I find difficult to express.

'Something to Declare', as above

The influence of Beckett

Waiting for Godot — there's just no telling what sort of effect it had on our society, who wrote because of it, or wrote in a different way because of it. But it really redefined the minima of theatrical experience. Up to then you had to have X; suddenly you had X minus one. Of course it would be absurd to deny my enormous debt to it, and love for it. To me the representative attitude is 'I am a human nothing.' Beckett qualifies as he goes along. He picks up a proposition and then dismantles and qualifies each part of its structure as he goes along, until he nullifies what he started out with. Beckett gives me more pleasure than I can express because he always ends up with a man surrounded by the wreckage of a proposition he had made in confidence only two minutes before.

'Something to Declare', as above

Against realism and the autobiographical

I simply don't like very much revealing myself. I am a very private sort of person. . . . Autobiographical work would tend to be on a realistic level since one's life is lived on a realistic level, and it happens that I am not any longer very interested in writing realistic drama. Now, do I not write realistic drama because I don't like to reveal myself autobiographically, or do I not reveal myself autobiographically because I don't like writing realistic drama? I would say the former.

Interview in *Behind the Scenes*

I write plays because writing dialogue is the only respectable way of contradicting yourself. I'm the kind of person who embarks on an endless leapfrog down the great moral issues. I put a position, rebut it, refute the rebuttal, and rebut the refutation. Forever. Endlessly. . . . We live in an age where the leper is the don't-know. It gets to be like binary roulette. You go by gut instinct. I don't respect people who are rigorously consistent. I like people who repudiate everything they've written every five years.

Mel Gussow, 'Stoppard Refutes Himself, Endlessly', p. 54

Drama and social comment

There is no such thing as 'pure' art — art is a commentary on something else in life — it might be adultery in the suburbs, or the Vietnamese war. I think that art ought to involve itself in contemporary social and political history as much as anything else, but I find it deeply embarrassing when large claims are made for such involvement: when, because art takes notice of something important, it's claimed that art is important. It's not. We are talking about marginalia   the top tiny fraction of the whole edifice. When Auden said his poetry didn't save one Jew from the gas chamber, he'd said it all. Basically I think that the most committed theatre in the land — I suppose that might be the Royal Court — has got about as much to do with events in the political area as the Queen's Theatre in Shaftesbury Avenue. I've never felt this — that art is important. That's been my secret guilt. I think it's the secret guilt of most artists.

Janet Watts, 'Tom Stoppard',
The Guardian, 21 Mar. 1973, p. 12

On Pinter

Pinter invented something — not the poetry of ordinary conversation that he is usually credited with, but the notion that you do not necessarily believe what people tell you in a theatre. Formerly you did so, unless there was reason for scepticism — as in an Agatha Christie play. In Pinter's plays there is no surface reason for not telling the truth, but he has persuaded an entire generation of theatregoers that people are not necessarily telling the truth, even when they have no reason for not doing so. He broke the first rule of the theatre: that you do not betray the audience.

T.E. Kalem, 'Ping Pong Philosopher',
Time, 6 May 1974, p. 55

Ideas and Comedy

What I try to do, is to end up by contriving the perfect marriage between the play of ideas and farce or perhaps even high comedy. Now, whether this is a desirable objective, or why it should be, is a matter which I'm not in the least interested in going into. But it *is* the objective, and to that end I have been writing plays which are farcical and without an idea in their funny heads, and I have also written plays which are all mouth, like *The Gamblers*, and don't bring off the comedy. And occasionally, I think *Jumpers* would be an example, I've got fairly close to a play which works as a funny play and which makes coherent, in terms of theatre, a fairly complicated intellectual argument.

'Ambushes for the Audience', *Theatre Quarterly*

On Max Frisch and Friedrich Dürrenmatt

When it comes to plays which are making a historical or social point, my preference is towards those which do it in metaphor. Take, for example, *The Fire Raisers*, by Frisch. . . . The reason, I think, must be that Frisch was struck by this metaphor of the firebugs rather as one might be struck by lightning, and it was that which inspired him to write the play. It is a perfect analogy and it explains as much really about how the Nazis were allowed to happen as does *The Rise and Fall of the Third Reich*. . . . I refer back to *The Visit* [by Dürrenmatt] many times as the summation of self-interest in life. When it becomes a matter of survival and economics, money is at the root of so much that we live by. I thought that was a beautifully wrought play. . . . It said something about democracy as well, and the point it was making is that democracy isn't an absolute good. If one has the democratic vote to do evil, then the principle of democracy is discredited.

'Interview with Tom Stoppard', Lewis Funke,
Playwrights Talk about Writing (Chicago, 1975), p. 228-9

Social comment in theatre

I tend to overreact against the large claims of committed theatre, so-called, because it is an ill-afforded luxury for an artist to convince himself that he has effectively done his bit because he grapples with important problems. The effect of art on society is very long-term and each artist is only a tiny part of that effect. For short-term effects, television journalism is a hundred times more effective. If I wanted to convince a million people that Inter Action should be given a million pounds, then I could hardly do worse than write a play — I should get on the *Eamonn Andrews Show*. A play is important only if it's good work, I've stopped being defensive about this. I used to feel out on a limb because when I started to write you were a shit if you weren't writing about Vietnam or housing. Now I have no compunction about that. To avert indirectly to *Travesties*, *The Importance of Being Earnest* is important but it says nothing about anything.

'Serious Frivolity', *Time Out*,
18-24 June 1976, p. 7

On his new interest in social issues

Sixteen years ago, when I first started writing plays, one was surrounded by artists who were making positive statements about social and political questions. But they did not seem to be aware of the difficulties involved in solving those questions. I had a reaction against making heroes for plays who had positive points of view and no qualifications about them. . . . But I was always morally, if not politically, involved. . . . There was no sudden conversion on the road to Damascus. I know human rights have been around for a long time and I have always been concerned with the daily horrors that I read in the newspapers.

'The Politicizing of Tom Stoppard,' p. 3

His interest in ideas

I'm not a playwright who is interested in character with a capital K and psychology with a capital S. I'm a playwright interested in ideas and forced to invent characters to express those ideas. All my people speak the same way, with the same cadences and sentence structures. When I write an African president into a play [*Night and Day*], I have to contrive to make him the only African president who speaks like me.

'Stoppard's Intellectual Cartwheels Now with Music', p. 22

Conventional structure in the plays

My plays don't break rules. If you take the orchestra away from
Every Good Boy, it is a series of scenes telling a coherent story
. . . I think I have more in common with Rattigan than with
Robert Wilson. We attempt to be coherent tellers of tales. In
Travesties a lot of odd things happen, but the crucial thing is that
the whole play is filtered through the memory of an old man and
the audience knows it. . . . Plays are events rather than texts.
They're written to happen, not to be read.

'Stoppard's Intellectual Cartwheels Now with Music',
as above

Working methods

The drafts of my plays would reveal quite banal versions; I just
sort of slap down something to remind me what I want to say. I
work slowly — my productivity is low, as the current jargon has
it. I am quite happy if I work a ten-hour day and end up with
two pages; I am pleased if I end up with one. I'm pleased — it's
okay. . . . I find it quite an alarming way of life when I am into
a play because I live in terror of its escaping somehow. You
know, each day is a sort of new beginning. I rarely sit down
knowing what I want to do next. And I feel that it is something
of a miracle to get to the end of a play. I can hardly believe that
it all worked out. There is no sense of inevitability about it.

Nancy Shields Hardin, 'An Interview with Tom Stoppard',
p. 156-7

Writers and issues

An American or British writer has no duty whatsoever to use his
work. He has the right to be an adornment or an entertainment.
He has no obligation except to write well. Whether that satisfies
him is a different question. What happens is that writers play their
strong suits. They express their temperaments. In England writers
feel no preoccupation to address themselves to political matters.
But people of a certain generation do. David Hare writes political
plays, but he would be political if he weren't writing plays. . . .
The situation gets more complicated if you are a writer in a totalitarian state. In a society that isn't free the compulsion to write
about being free is so strong that to say it's an obligation is
irrelevant. . . .

'Stoppard Debates the Role of the Writer', p. 13

a: Primary Sources

The shorter plays are collected in three volumes: *The Dog It Was that Died and Other Plays* (London: Faber, 1973); *Four Plays for Radio;* and *Squaring the Circle/ Every Good Boy Deserves Favour/Professional Foul* (London: Faber, 1984). Publication details of individual plays may be found under their titles in Section 2.

Articles and Essays

'A Very Satirical Thing Happened to Me on the Way to the Theatre Tonight', *Encore*, X (Mar.-Apr. 1963), p. 33-6.

'Just Impossible', *Plays and Players*, Jan. 1967, p. 28-9. [Review of *The Impossible Years*, by Bob Fisher and Arthur Marx.]

'A Case of Vice Triumphant', *Plays and Players*, Mar. 1967, p. 16-9. [Review of *The Soldier's Fortune*, by Thomas Otway, Royal Court.]

'The Definite Maybe', *The Author*, LXXVIII (Spring 1967), p. 18-20. [His career as a writer.]

'Something to Declare', *Sunday Times*, 25 Feb. 1968, p. 47. [Useful piece, including discussion of his dependence on his subconscious; his love of language and Beckett; possibilities of theatre.]

'Joker as Artist', *Sunday Times*, 11 Oct. 1970, p. 40. [Review of *Magritte*, by Suzi Gablik.]

'In Praise of Pedantry', *Punch*, 14 July 1971, p. 62-3.

'Orghast', *Times Literary Supplement*, 1 Oct. 1971, p. 1174. [On the language Ted Hughes invented for a performance by Peter Brook's company at Shiraz Festival; Stoppard draws on his interview with Hughes and on seeing part of the show in rehearsal.]

'Yes, We Have No Banana', *The Guardian*, 10 Dec. 1971, p. 10. [Amusing piece on working simultaneously on *Jumpers* for the National Theatre, and on *Dogg's Our Pet* on the fringe.]

'Playwrights and Professors', *Times Literary Supplement*, 13 Oct. 1972, p. 1219. [Attacks 'writing-about-writing', especially drama criticism, which is usually remote from the theatre and unhelpful to practitioners.]

Review, *A Supplement to the Oxford English Dictionary, Vol. 1: A-G, Punch*, 13 Dec. 1972, p. 893-4.

'Acting out the Oil Game', *Observer*, 8 Sept. 1974, p. 24; 'The Miss UK Sales Promotion', 15 Sept. 1974, p. 27; 'Disaster in Bangladesh,' 22 Sept. 1974, p. 27; 'Festival of Soap Opera', 29 Sept. 1974, p. 28. [Television reviews. 'It is worth preserving the distinction between serious work and carpentry, for it is not merely a distinction put about by guilty intellectuals secretly hooked on *Crossroads* and *Coronation Street*. . . . The real charge to be made against the high-output serials is that they seldom rise to anything as true as a clash of personalities — they merely manipulate types through a concatenation of plot-lines and cliff-hangers.' (29 Sept.)]

'Dirty Linen in Prague', *New York Times*, 11 Feb. 1977, Sec. I, p. 27.

'The Face at the Window', *Sunday Times*, 27 Feb. 1977, p. 33. [His visit to Russian dissidents.]

'But for the Middle Classes', *Times Literary Supplement*, 3 June 1977, p. 677. [Review of *Enemies of Society*, by Paul Johnson. 'Truth is objective. Civilization is the pursuit of truth in freedom.' Stoppard appears to identify with 'the western liberal democracy favouring an intellectual elite and a progressive middle class and based on a moral order derived from Christian absolutes'.]

'Prague: the Story of the Chartists', *New York Review of Books*, 4 Aug. 1977, p. 11-5.

'Looking-Glass World', *New Statesman*, 28 Oct. 1977, p. 571-2. [Havel and other dissident Czech writers.]

'Tom Stoppard on the KGB's Olympic Trials', *Sunday Times*, 6 Apr. 1980, p. 16. [The Olympic Games boycott is an 'unrepeatable opportunity' for the West to show its support for Russian dissidents such as Vladimir Borisov.]

'Prague's Wall of Silence', *The Times*, 18 Nov. 1981, p. 10.

'Wildlife Observed: the Galapagos: Paradise and Purgatory', *Observer Magazine*, 29 Nov. 1981, p. 38-51.

Is it True What They Say about Shakespeare? OUP: International Shakespeare Association Occasional Paper, No. 2, 1982. [Shakespeare's genius is a gift for 'verbal cadences' and the ability 'to observe human nature with a clear eye and to understand human behaviour with an unclouded mind'.]

'Open Letter to President Husak', *They Shoot Writers, Don't They?*, ed. George Theiner (London: Faber, 1984), p. 57-9. [On Czechoslovakia's refusal to give him a visa for a visit.]

Interviews

Dan Sullivan, 'Young British Playwright Here for Rehearsal of *Rosencrantz*', *New York Times*, 27 Aug. 1967, p. 27.

'Tom Stoppard', in *Behind the Scenes*, ed. Joseph McCrindle (London: Pitman, 1971). [Interview with Giles Gordon, reprinted from *Transatlantic Review*, No. 29 (Summer 1968).]

Mel Gussow, 'Stoppard Refutes Himself, Endlessly', *New York Times*, 26 Apr. 1972, p. 54.

Janet Watts, 'Tom Stoppard', *The Guardian*, 21 Mar. 1973, p. 12.

Under Bow Bells: Dialogues with Joseph McCullough (London: Sheldon Press, 1974), p. 162-70.

T.E. Kalem, 'Ping Pong Philosopher', *Time*, 6 May 1974, p. 55.

'Ambushes for the Audience', *Theatre Quarterly*, May-July 1974, p. 3-17; reprinted in *New Theatre Voices of the Seventies*, ed. Simon Trussler (London: Eyre Methuen, 1981), p. 58-69.

Mark Amory, 'The Joke's the Thing', *Sunday Times Magazine*, 9 June 1974, p. 65, 67-8, 71-2, 74

Lewis Funke, 'Interview with Tom Stoppard', in *Playwrights Talk about Writing* (Chicago: Dramatic Publishing Co., 1975), p. 218-31.

Mel Gussow, 'Playwright, Star Provide a Little Curtain Raiser', *New York Times*, 31 Oct. 1975, p. 21.

Steve Grant, 'Serious Frivolity', *Time Out*, 18-24 June 1976, p. 7.

Ronald Hayman, *Tom Stoppard* (London: Heinemann, 1977). [Includes two interviews, which took place in 1974 and 1976.]

John Leonard, 'Tom Stoppard Tries on a "Knickers Farce",' *New York Times*, 9 Jan. 1977, Sec. II, p. 1.

Jon Bradshaw, 'Tom Stoppard: Nonstop Word Games with a Hit Playwright', *New York*, 10 Jan. 1977, p. 47-51.

Jon Bradshaw, 'Tom Stoppard Non-Stop', *Sunday Telegraph Magazine*, 26 June 1977, p. 29-30, 32, 34.

Milton Shulman, 'The Politicizing of Tom Stoppard', *New York Times*, 23 Apr. 1978, Sec. II, p. 3, 27.

Hugh Hebert, 'A Playwright in Undiscovered Country', *The Guardian*, 7 July 1979, p. 10.

Mel Gussow, 'Stoppard's Intellectual Cartwheels Now with Music', *New York Times*, 29 July 1979, Sec. II, p. 1, 22.

Robert Berkvist, 'This Time, Stoppard Plays It (Almost) Straight', *New York Times*, 25 Nov. 1979, Sec. II, p. 1, 5.

Joost Kuurman, 'An Interview with Tom Stoppard', *Dutch Quarterly Review*, X (1980), p. 41-57.

Nancy Shields Hardin, 'An Interview with Tom Stoppard',

Contemporary Literature, XXII (Spring 1981), p. 153-66.

David Gollob and David Roper, 'Trad Tom Pops in', *Gambit*, No. 37 (Summer 1981), p. 5-17.

Pendennis, 'Dialogue with a Driven Man', *The Observer*, 30 Aug. 1981, p. 18.

Mel Gussow, 'The Real Tom Stoppard', *New York Times Magazine*, 1 Jan. 1984, p. 18-23, 28.

Samuel G. Freedman, 'Stoppard Debates the Role of the Writer', *New York Times*, 20 Feb. 1984, Sec. C, p. 13.

b: Secondary Sources

Full-length Studies

C.W.E. Bigsby, *Tom Stoppard*. Harlow: Longmans, for British Council, enlarged ed., 1979.

Michael Billington, *Stoppard the Playwright*. London: Methuen, 1985.

Tim Brassell, *Tom Stoppard: an Assessment*. London: Macmillan, 1985.

Victor L. Cahn, *Beyond Absurdity: the Plays of Tom Stoppard*. Rutherford, N.J.: Farleigh Dickinson University Press, 1979.

Richard Corballis, *Stoppard: the Mystery and the Clockwork*. Oxford: Amber Lane, 1984.

Joan Fitzpatrick Dean, *Tom Stoppard: Comedy as a Moral Matrix*. Columbia, Missouri: University of Missouri Press, 1981.

Lucina Paquet Gabbard, *The Stoppard Plays*. Troy, N.Y.: Whitston, 1982.

Ronald Hayman, *Tom Stoppard*. London: Heinemann, enlarged ed., 1979.

Jim Hunter, *Tom Stoppard's Plays*. London: Faber, 1982.

Felicia Hardison Londré, *Tom Stoppard*. New York: Ungar, 1981.

Thomas R. Whitaker, *Tom Stoppard*. London: Macmillan ('Modern Dramatists' Series), 1983.

Articles and Chapters in Books

Jill L. Levenson, 'Views from a Revolving Door: Tom Stoppard's Canon to Date', *Queens Quarterly*, LVIII (1971), p. 431-42.

John Russell Taylor, *The Second Wave* (London: Methuen, 1971), p. 94-107.

William Babula, 'The Play-Life Metaphor in Shakespeare and Stoppard', *Modern Drama*, XV (Winter 1972), p. 279-81.

Gillian Farish, 'Into the Looking-Glass Bowl: an Instant of Grateful Terror', *University of Windsor Review*, X (1975), p. 14-29.

Clive James, 'Count Zero Splits the Infinite: Tom Stoppard's Plays', *Encounter*, XLV (Nov. 1975), p. 68-76.

Julian Gitzen, 'Tom Stoppard: Chaos in Perspective', *Southern Humanities Review*, X (1976), p. 143-52.

Brian M. Crossley, 'An Investigation of Stoppard's "Hound" and "Foot" ', *Modern Drama*, XX (Mar. 1977), p. 77-86.

Oleg Kerensky, *The New British Drama* (London: Hamilton, 1977), p. 145-71.

Gabriele S. Robinson, 'Plays without Plot: the Theatre of Tom Stoppard', *Educational Theatre Journal*, XXIX (Mar. 1977), p. 37-48.

Thomas R. Whitaker, *Fields of Plays in Modern Drama* (Princeton, N.J.: Princeton University Press, 1977), p. 9-34.

Philip Roberts, 'Tom Stoppard: Serious Artist or Siren?', *Critical Quarterly*, XX (1978), p. 84-92.

Alfred Schwarz, *From Büchner to Beckett* (Athens, Ohio: Ohio University Press, 1978), p. 325-32.

Andrew Kennedy, 'Natural, Mannered, and Parodic Dialogue', *Yearbook of English Studies*, IX (1979), p. 28-54.

Eric Salmon, 'Faith in Tom Stoppard', *Queens Quarterly*, LXXXVI (1979), p. 215-32.

June Schlueter, *Metafictional Characters in Modern Drama* (New York: Columbia University Press, 1979).

Hersh Zeifman, 'Tomfoolery: Stoppard's Theatrical Puns', *Yearbook of English Studies*, IX (1979), p. 204-20; reprinted in *Modern British Dramatists: New Perspectives*, ed. John Russell Brown (Englewood Cliffs, N.J.: Prentice-Hall, 1984), p. 85-108.

B.S. Levy, 'Serious Propositions Compromised by Frivolity', *Critical Quarterly*, XXII (Autumn 1980), p. 79-85.

Bobbi Rothstein, 'The Reappearance of Public Man: Stoppard's *Jumpers* and *Professional Foul*', *Kansas Quarterly*, XII (1980), p. 35-44.

Kenneth Tynan, *Show People* (London: Weidenfeld, 1980), p. 44-123.

Normand Berlin, *The Secret Cause* (Amherst: University of Massachusetts Press, 1981), p. 65-86.

Enoch Brater, 'Parody, Travesty and Politics in the Plays of Tom Stoppard', in *Essays on Contemporary British Drama*, ed. Hedwig Bock and Albert Wertheim (Munich: Max Hueber, 1981), p. 117-30. Also contains Dietrich Schwanitz, 'The Method of Madness: Tom Stoppard's Theatrum Logico-Philosophicum', p. 131-54.

Ruby Cohn, 'Tom Stoppard: Light Dramas and Dirges in Marriage', in *Contemporary English Drama*, ed. C.W.E. Bigsby (London: Edward Arnold, 1981), p. 109-20.

Dougald McMillan, 'Dropping the Other Boot', *Gambit*, No. 37 (1981), p. 61-76.

Arthur M. Salzman, 'Tom Stoppard Joins the Fray', *Theatre Annual*, XXVI (1981), p. 68-80.

'Juggler to the British Stage', *The Observer*, 14 Nov. 1982, p. 7.

Mary R. Davison, 'Transcending Logic: Stoppard, Wittgenstein and Aristophanes', in *Alogical Modern Drama*, ed. Kenneth S. White (Amsterdam: Rodopi, 1982), p. 39-60.

Andrew Kennedy, 'Tom Stoppard's Dissident Comedies', *Modern Drama*, XXV (Dec. 1982), p. 469-76.

Benedict Nightingale, *An Introduction to Fifty Modern British Plays* (London: Pan, 1982), p. 405-22.

Robert Wilcher, 'Tom Stoppard and the Art of Communication', *Journal of Beckett Studies*, No. 8 (1982), p. 105-23.

Anne Wright, 'Tom Stoppard', in *British Dramatists since World War II,* ed. Stanley Weintraub (Detroit: Gale, 1982), p. 482-500.

Roger Scruton, 'The Real Stoppard', *Encounter*, LX (Feb. 1983), p. 44-7.

Keir Elam, 'After Magritte, After Carroll, After Wittgenstein: What Tom Stoppard's Tortoise Taught Us', *Modern Drama*, XXVII (Dec. 1984), p. 469-85.

John Russell Taylor, 'From *Rosencrantz* to *The Real Thing*', *Plays and Players*, Oct. 1984, p. 13-16.

Reference Sources

Randolph Ryan, 'Theatre Checklist No. 2: Tom Stoppard', *Theatrefacts*, No. 2 (May-July 1974), p. 3-9.

Kimball King, *Twenty Modern British Playwrights: a Bibliography, 1956 to 1976* (New York: Garland, 1977), p. 217-30.

Charles A. Carpenter, 'Bond, Shaffer, Stoppard, Storey: an International Checklist of Commentary', *Modern Drama*, XXIV (Dec. 1981), p. 551-5.

David Bratt, *Tom Stoppard: a Reference Guide*. Boston: G.K. Hall, 1982.